SKYSCRAPER ARCHITECTS

SKYSCRAPER ARCHITECTS

Coordination and texts
Ariadna Àlvarez Garreta, architect

Translation
Mark Holloway

Design and typesetting
Manel Peret Calderón

Director of production
Juanjo Rodríguez Novel

Copyright © 2004 Atrium Group

Published by: Atrium Group de ediciones y publicaciones, S.L.
c/ Ganduxer, 112
08022 BARCELONA

Tel: +34 932 540 099
Fax: +34 932 118 139
e-mail: atrium@atriumgroup.org
www.atriumbooks.com

ISBN: 84-95692-40-6
Dep. Legal: B-29270-2004

Printed in Spain
GRABASA

THE ARCHITECTURE OF SKYSCRAPERS AT THE DAWNING OF THE NEW MILLENNIUM

Since 1890, when, in the USA, the term skyscraper was first used to refer to office buildings with a large number of floors, an intense social debate between the architectural world and public opinion has been stirred up. Skyscrapers are an all-American product and fruit of the 20th century and their presence and evolution has always been a symbol of technological advancement, the consumer society and liberal politics.

The first skyscrapers raised in the city of Chicago in 1980 were purely functional buildings. They responded to technical and economic factors and architecture, in its purest sense, was pushed into the background. Once this initial 'engineering' phase had been overcome, the search for style began. As a result, architects started to seek inspiration in the past of western civilization which led to an adaptation of Greek temples, belfries, Renaissance palaces and vertical castles. With the coming of the 50's, Modernism put an end to this historicist style with a complete revolution. A skyscraper started to be considered a creative challenge and a coherent response to go along with technological and cultural development was demanded from the architects.

Since this decade, this style of architecture has been taken up in Europe and Asia whenever cities have felt the need to enlarge their floor space and to create financial centers to symbolize their potential. And it is that skyscrapers are not only functional constructions, but they are forms of artistic expression as well. As such, they still present a series of unresolved problems that along with their physical impact on their urban surroundings make them one of the most defiant challenges for an architect.

The formal and technical evolution of skyscrapers and workspaces has always gone along side by side in a historical context. Throughout the 20th century, technical advances such as elevators, steel structural systems, coverings based on lightweight glass curtain-walls, fluorescent lighting and the generalized use of air conditioning, among other things, have enabled the construction of higher and higher buildings. This has led to greater efficiency, productivity and benefits for the companies that use them.

All of these changes, in addition to the technological ones (such as the fax, the computer, electronic mail, cellular telephones and video conferencing), have accompanied the evolution and change in the field of the spatial design of offices. The development of mass production standardized the design of spaces and furnishings. The result of this, particularly as of World War II, encouraged a rigid and modular image of work that did not evolve until the 60's. In this period, the development of certain fields, such as human relations or psychology, helped to establish offices as a formative environment for workers. Along with this, the open plan office with flexible spaces and furnishings to attend the diverse demands of the users was born. This practice has been maintained to the present day. New concepts have also been introduced such as virtual workspaces and environmental compatibility which has led to the necessity of establishing physical places to develop work activities and to extend urban activity to other parts such as rural nuclei.

It was not until little more than a decade ago that the consequences of the environmental impact of these buildings upon the city were first considered by the public at large and above all by the profes-

8

sional sector. Architects and developers have become sensitive to the need to assume a responsibility for the environment that integrates the principles of sustainable architecture and responsible design. Architects such as Dr Kenneth Yeang from Asia; Norman Foster, Richard Rogers and Renzo Piano from Europe; Fox & Fowle, César Pelli, KPF and Murphy/Jahn from North America (to mention a few who are included in this book) illustrate this philosophy that will be indispensable in the decades to come.

This volume proposes a review of the skyscrapers that open the new millennium. It focuses on how their authors have dealt with architecture in relationship with society and the city and in what ways they have resolved the design problems posed by these buildings. Buildings projected and/or built between the last decade of the 20th century and the beginning of the 21st by leading architects from all over the world have been selected. In this way, buildings that form part of the architectural debate of this new millennium are shown. In these, the aim is no longer to demonstrate technique, but to search for formal and technical solutions in buildings of height so that they are sustainable, able to improve the quality of life of the people who inhabit them and to maintain a dialogue with the city.

The terrorist attack of September 11, 2001 on the Twin Towers in New York has established a before and after in the artistic, political, and social debate on skyscrapers and has brought into question not only the extent to which they should perhaps be limited, but even if they should exist. The reconstruction of Ground Zero is a clear example of the division of opinion among architects, developers and society at large over an age-old question that can be well illustrat-

ed by the fable of the tower of Babel and the fact that of the seven schemes presented, four proposed constructing the highest building in the world over the ruins of the towers. Among them, the winning project from Daniel Libeskind which presents a skyscraper as the best way to create spaces for parks and an area for reflection as required by the program can be found.

His project consists of a 540-meter-high glass needle as a central axis for the Memorial Foundations of the World Trade Center (a group of retail and cultural buildings) which, along with the Statue of Liberty, is to give a welcome to the city of New York and to North American culture. It has been more than two decades since a building as high as the Twin Towers, 110 floors and 417 meters high projected by the architect M Yamasaki in 1964, has been built in the United States. It is also considered difficult to justify the construction of a building more than 80 floors high other than for purely symbolic motives. September 11 will not impede the building of skyscrapers, but certainly should provoke a sincere reflection upon the growth of cities during the coming years.

Present predictions for our planet's population growth are high. Cities will lose their traditional scale in terms of urban nuclei (recognizable forms) and they will become complex megacities as a result of the fusion of numerous centers. What kind of society will inhibit these cities and what influence this urban development will have over its inhabitants is a responsibility that cannot be eluded.

ARIADNA ÀLVAREZ GARRETA

9

Norman Foster was born in 1935 in Manchester where he studied architecture. He established his own studio of architecture and urban development in 1967 in London along with four associates: Spencer de Grey, David Nelson, Ken Shuttleworth and Graham Phillips. The philosophy of the studio is summarized by the spatial conception of its offices. These are located in a large open space with no subdivisions so that a positive working environment that encourages teamwork is created.

The tasks undertaken by the studio range from large scale projects, such as Hong Kong's new airport, to the design of the doorknobs for the same building or to the planning of urban infrastructures, buildings, interiors and exhibitions. They have built all over the world, from England to the Scandinavian peninsula, the United States, Hong Kong, Japan, Malaysia, Arabia Saudi and Australia.

Norman Foster was honored with a life peerage, taking the title Lord Foster of Thames Bank, in 1999 and has received prestigious prizes such as the Royal Gold Medal (1983), the AIA Gold Medal (1994) and the Pritzker Prize (1999).

www.fosterandpartners.com

1986	Hong Kong & Shanghai Bank Headquarters, Hong Kong
1990	Apartment Building Riverside Three, Battersea (London)
1991	Century tower, Tokyo
1992	Torre de Telecomunicaciones de Collserola (Barcelona)
1993	Carre dArt (Musuem of Contemporary Art), Nimes
1995	Bilbao Metro
1997	Commerzbank Headquarters, Frankfurt
1999	Reichstag, Germany's New Parliament, Berlin
2000	British Museum Great Court, London
2004	Swiss Re Headquarters, London

NORMAN FOSTER
Foster & Partners

FOSTER
PART 1

FOSTER
PART 1

Architect:
FOSTER & PARTNERS
Developer:
Obayashi Corporation
Structural Engineering:
Obayashi Corporation
Situation:
Tokyo (Japan)
Project Date:
1989
Floors:
170
Height:
840 m
Use:
Offices, residencies and services
Photography:
Richard Davies

Tokyo is a megalopolis that, as indicated by present forecasts, will see an increase in population of more than fifteen million inhabitants by the year 2020. The Millennium Tower confronts the growth of the cities of the future and proposes solutions to the social challenges created by urban expansion. Particularly in Tokyo, where the shortage of land will bring construction to a halt in the city, alternative solutions will have to be found bearing in mind the additional problem that Japan is an island. This project, the most futuristic projected by Norman Foster since the 70's and 80's when he developed proposals along with his fellow architect Buckminster Fuller, was commissioned in 1989 by the Japanese corporation Obayashi.

It concerned the promotion of 1,040,000 m2 of living spaces, offices and commercial areas that was to gain two kilometers of land from the sea near the Bay of Tokyo. A 170-floor conical tower was proposed (twice the height of the highest tower in the world at that time) surrounded by a spiral steel network that would contain everything necessary to enable a community of 60,000 people to develop an autonomous life. This great house, which contains a vertical city, is self-sufficient. It produces its own energy. It processes its waste materials and has its own transportation system: a high-speed metro that circulates horizontally and vertically in convoys for 160 people. The metro stops every thirty floors in intermediate spaces or sky centers from which further displacements are resolved at a different rhythm using stairs and elevators. Each of these centers occupies five floors that they are connected by means of terraces, gardens and intermediate levels that give a sense of place and personality. Each one has been designed according to the function it is to fulfill be it a hotel or large retail center. The remaining floors are grouped in various levels that form units. Offices and services are located in the lower levels and, as the tower gains height, living spaces become available. The functional approach of the building is along the lines of a city formed by floors grouped

&

NE

MILLENNIUM

13

in vertical neighborhoods and it is intended that each one of these possesses its own personality. This is achieved by locating differing complementary services and activities within the living areas such as restaurants and lookout points that command the most spectacular views. At the base of the tower, a marina is located that is connected to the coast by a bridge.

Given the high seismic activity in Japan and the great height of the tower, special attention has been paid to how the building may respond to any kind of movement in the earth. As a result, the conical structure of the tower and its structural encasement make it completely stable. On the one hand, the top section is not habitable and only contains equipment so, in terms of weight, it is light, open to the elements and resistant to horizontal forces. On the other hand, as we approach the base of the building, the section increases in diameter and consequently there is greater solidity and stability. This project, which finally did not come to be built, evokes the utopias of the North American architect F. Lloyd Wright's one mile tower and the urban fantasies of the English group Archigram in as much as it also represents a singular social utopia.

Photograph of the maquette that was presented along with the project. The conical building groups its floors in vertical communities the sum of which constitutes a city.

Top. Plan locating the situation of accesses and the marina. Bottom. Floor plans of the tower that rises over an artificial island surrounded by a marina connected to the coast by a bridge.

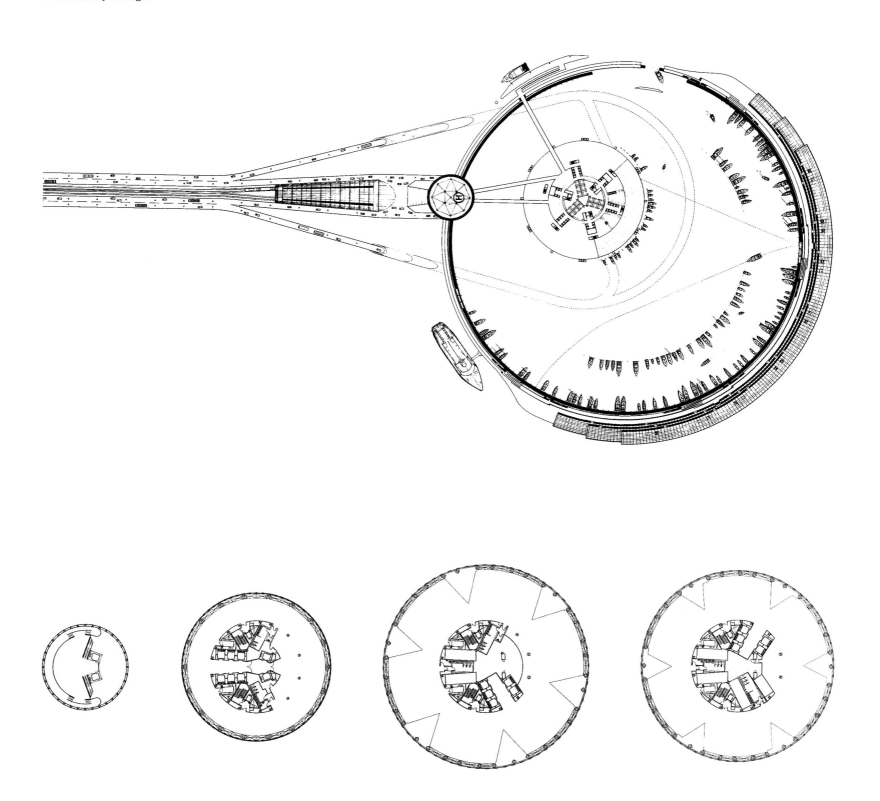

From left to right: view of the tower, elevation and cross-section of the building.

Various views of the maquette in
which its cladding is shown
(a mesh of helical steel) and a
detail of the bridge that connects
it to the bay of Tokyo.
To the right, a drawing shows
an ideal view of the project.

FOSTER
PARTI

Architect:

FOSTER & PARTNERS

Developer:

Commerzbank AG

Structural Engineering:

Ove Arup & Partners

Situation:

Frankfurt, Germany

Project Date:

1991

Completion Date:

1997

Floors:

53

Height:

259 m

Use:

Offices

Photography:

Ian Lambot

Nigel Young

Commerzbank's new headquarters is not only the first "green" office tower built to date in Europe, but it is also the highest. This project won an international competition in 1991 due to its innovative character in the environmental field and to its exploration of new ideas for workspaces in office buildings.

The building has been constructed over a triangular base and as the vertical communications nuclei, services and structure have been displaced toward the perimeter, each of the sides forms an open space and the center, being completely free from obstruction, a large empty expanse. This central area forms a great atrium that relates and connects all the levels of the building visually. The different levels can also be illuminated and ventilated in a natural way. Mechanical means (fan coils or similar) are unnecessary as natural air currents are created. Also, all the workplaces are guaranteed to be close to a facade as each side of the triangle has two facades: the interior to the atrium and the exterior to the city. Each multi-leveled group forms a unit and, between each of these units, hanging gardens, various floors high, have been inserted. In addition to functioning as rest zones for the users of the building, they provide views of the workplaces. Having fragmented the building, consumption and energy saving schemes can be administrated more efficiently. This permits each user to regulate the environmental conditions of his or her own office, according to his or her needs, in a more positive and relaxing working climate. This distances the building from environmental influences such as acoustic contamination.

The facade is a double skin that offers protection from excessive solar radiation in summer, but, however, allows it to penetrate in winter. This is achieved by means of adjustable screens which prevent glare and the sensation of sultriness. The hanging gardens, along with the structure and the functional disposition of the construction, are a characteristic

© Ian Lambot

COMMERZBANK HEADQUARTERS

element in the composition of the facade of the Commerzbank building. They break the continuity of a vertical plane and offer a modern image of transparency and luminosity in the building.

Urbanistically, the image of the building breaks down the forcible volume of a 53-story tower and as an attempt to reduce aggressiveness, the corners have been curved and a smaller facade surface offered by basing the building on a triangular floor plan. Along with steel, aluminum and glass, vegetation is found that, in accordance to the orientation of each side of the triangle, proceeds from North America, Asia or the Mediterranean area. This building, which has an important presence in the skyline of the city, maintains, however, a relationship with the stone buildings of smaller scale that form the texture of the city. It raises next to its ancestor (the first building to house this banking entity) in a central zone of Frankfurt, the European financial district, where the highest office buildings are found. Its construction led to the restructuring of the original building and the more immediate urban surroundings providing, on the ground floor, a great hall that presents a new public space where stores, restaurants, cafés and spaces to celebrate cultural and social events have been situated. Commerzbank wish to establish a model for sustainable buildings that serve as a link between the traditional urban structure and the urban community in the construction of the city of the 21st century.

Different zooms of the facade in which the window as an entity can be observed. The sum total of these form a self-supporting facade and modules of various floors create units which contain large window boxes for plants.

Top. Detail of a landscape-gardened
rest area in the interior of the building.
Bottom. Ariel photograph taken
during the construction of the
Commerzbank that can be seen
as a conceptual image
of the building.

© Nigel Young

Top. Detail of the interior skylight that provides natural lighting to the interior facades.
Bottom. Two views: one from street level and another from an elevated point in which we can observe how the tower coexists along with the traditional architecture of Frankfurt.

Top. Detail of the interior atrium
and the skylight.
Bottom. Detail of an interior garden
that fulfils various functions ranging
from establishing rest areas
to improving the working
conditions of those who work
in the building.

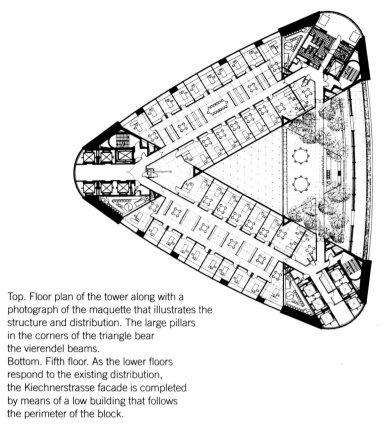

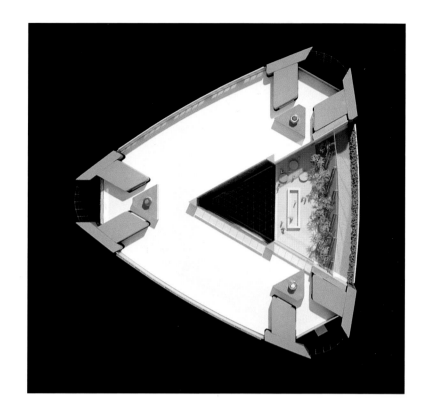

Top. Floor plan of the tower along with a photograph of the maquette that illustrates the structure and distribution. The large pillars in the corners of the triangle bear the vierendel beams.
Bottom. Fifth floor. As the lower floors respond to the existing distribution, the Kiechnerstrasse facade is completed by means of a low building that follows the perimeter of the block.

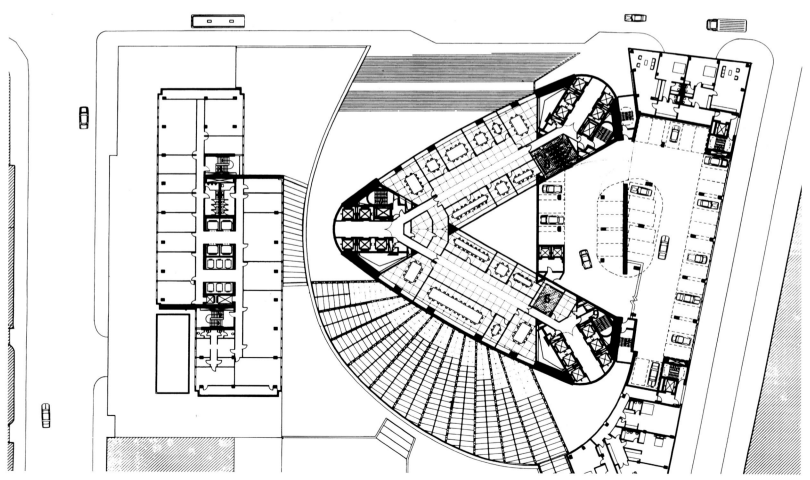

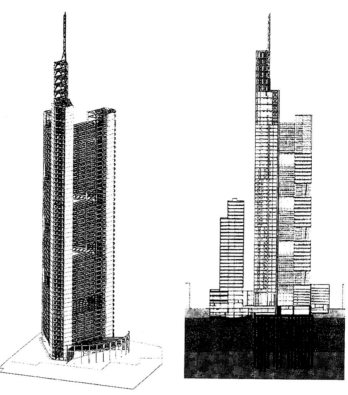

Top. Photograph of the tower
in the context of the city, axonometric
drawing and cross-section that shows
the grouping of various floors to form
units and the important foundations.
Bottom. Various scale models
from different phases
of the project.

Fox & Fowle Architects P.C. is a firm of architecture, interior design and urban development that was founded in 1978 by the architects Robert F. Fox and Bruce S. Fowle in New York.

The philosophy of the studio is based on the idea of collaboration with the client in a search for solutions that will fulfill the functional aspects of the assignment, resolve the esthetic requirements and establish a budget for the final project. The resulting building is to express the identity and the aspirations of the client and serve to enrich the human experience. They have also become well known for their concepts of ecological construction and sustainable architecture.

Their capacity to elaborate daring and innovative designs has been recognized through numerous publications in magazines and newspapers. They have participated in various national and international architectural contests. Recently, they have been awarded with the Medal of Honor of the AIA New York Chapter, two design prizes by the AIA New York State and an honorary prize by the Society of American Registered Architects.

www.foxfowle.com

1987	American Craft Museum, New York
1990	Office Building 1675 Broadway, New York
1990	Hotel Embassy Suites, New York
1992	Office Building 101 Avenue of the Americas, New York
1996	Addition, Renovation and Interiors of the American Bible Society, New York
1999	The Condé Nast Building, New York
2000	Industrial & Commercial Bank of China Building, Shanghai
2001	The Reuters Building, New York
2002	Times Square Subway Entrance, New York
2002	Shanghai Jahwa Tower, Shanghai

ROBERT F. FOX, BRUCE S.FOWLE
Fox & Fowle Architects P.C.

FOX & FO
FOX & FO
AR

Architect:

FOX & FOWLE ARCHITECTS P.C.

Developer:

The Durst Organization

Structural Engineering:

Canton Seinuk Group P.C.

Situation:

New York (New York, USA)

Project Date:

1997

Completion Date:

1999

Floors:

48

Height:

247 meters

Use:

Offices

Photography:

Andrew Gordon

The Condé Nast Building @ Four Times Square was the first building that was born out of the 42nd Street Master Plan. This plan was promoted by a consortium of mixed public and private interests called 42nd Street Development Corporation created by the state of New York for the reconstruction of the traditional center of Manhattan. This building has been followed by others such as the Reuters Building in 2001 (projected by the same architects) and E Walk by, also North American, Arquitectonica. The Condé Nast Building assignment supposed, for promoters and architects, going beyond the classical New York office building and taking, as a starting point, the building's relationship with the city and its dynamics. It was born to the calling of providing a new standard for the Manhattan of the 21st century and of capturing the essence of the commercial city as well as proposing a contemporary corporate image.

The building conforms to what pre-existed so that the treatment received by the exterior is by no means uniform. Although we find a coherent final volume as a result, each of the facades deals with its surroundings in a different way. The facades that give onto Broadway are composed of a metal and glass curtainwall that, interrupted by lines of neon at ground floor level, reflect the dynamic and boisterous character of Times Square. The corner is enclosed by a semi-cylinder eleven floors high that accommodates the Nasdaq headquarters. Here, a screen (that is, in fact, the outer covering of the building) displays a live transmission of the stock-market rates. The facades oriented toward 42nd Street are of masonry and reflect, with their color and texture, the seriousness of the financial district 'midtown' and the refined style of Bryant Park. In its upper section, the building reflects its structural system in its topping as well as housing, given its situation on the "crossroads of the world", resources of high technology.

From an environmental the point of view, this is a responsible building designed with the collaboration of various scientific institutes and the

CONDÉ NAST

Commission for the Defense of Natural Resources. All of the systems installed along with the construction technology employed have been evaluated so as to guarantee interior comfort, the impact on the health of the occupiers, environmental awareness and a reduction in the use of energy. As a consequence, the Condé Nast Building defines a new standard in construction processes and promotes the use of sustainable materials. The advanced design of the roof incorporates recycled energetic resources in photovoltaic panels. This building consumes 45% less energy annually than a traditional office block. A long time before the term "green" was incorporated into the dictionary of construction technology, the architects Robert F. Fox and Bruce S. Fowle were well-known for introducing measures to conserve energy, to maximize the use of natural light and to maintain the interior environments clean of contaminated air.

The Condé Nast Building gathers the essence of the city as testimony of a physical memory by juxtaposing planes and volumes that bring the more immediate scales and typologies of urban surroundings together. This mixture of images with historical, futuristic and commercial references, suggest a characteristic Times Square in an order of buildings and routine scenes that evoke another time. The collage of volumes and facades describe the energy the street possesses and an integrated composition that culminates in a highly energetic conclusion develops. This articulated top, marked by four screens illuminated by signs and crowned with a communications tower, perforates and radiates in the new skyline of the city of New York creating a memorable 'high tech' icon in the intersection of Broadway with 42nd Street.

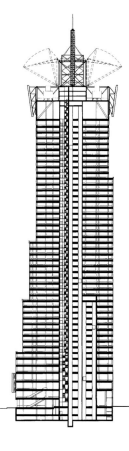

Top. The Condé Nast Building is situated in Times Square opposite another building by the same architects - the Reuters Building (to the left) completed in 2001.
Bottom right. Nocturnal image in which the building, due to its contemporary architecture, stands out among the classical buildings of Manhattan.
The architects, sensitive to the processes of urban planning and environmental factors, have designed a building that establishes a dialogue with the city and develops an integral and energetic concept.
Bottom right. Cross-section of the tower. The building is crowned by a series of panels and an antenna that, simultaneously, provide a formal and technical element.

Top. Level 48, or typical floor plan for the upper levels, which has a distribution based on the location of a central nucleus forming an open floor plan.
Bottom. Elevations of the tower in which the planes, compositions and figures that are established can be read. The building's topping is a technical composite element that distinguishes the building and relates it to the tradition of American skyscrapers.

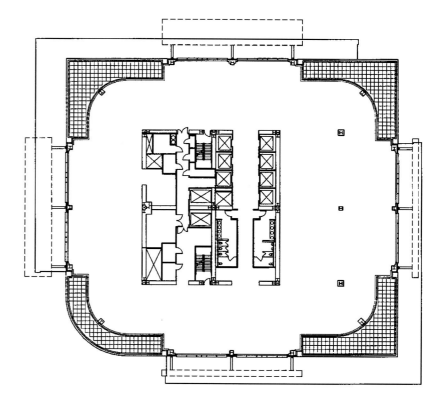

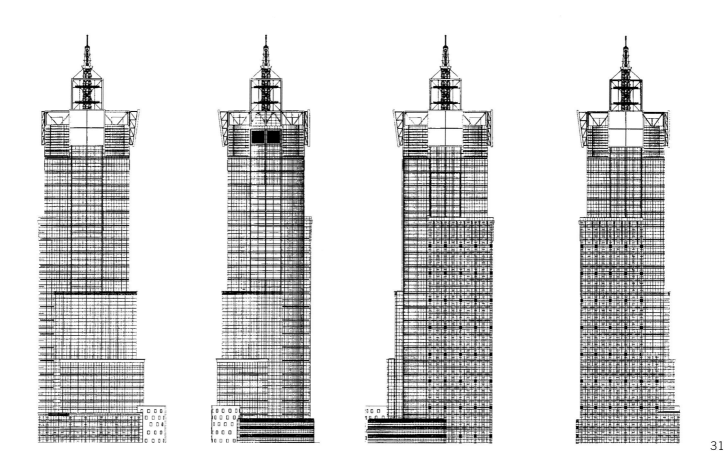

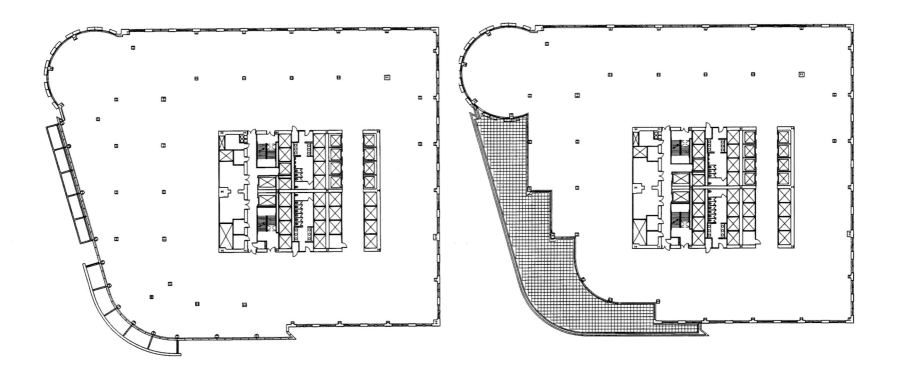

Top from left to right. Floor plans of the lower levels (in ascending order). Bottom. Nocturnal image of the tower, a point of reference in the center of Manhattan, the high-tech top of which is the icon of the intersection between Broadway and 42nd Street.

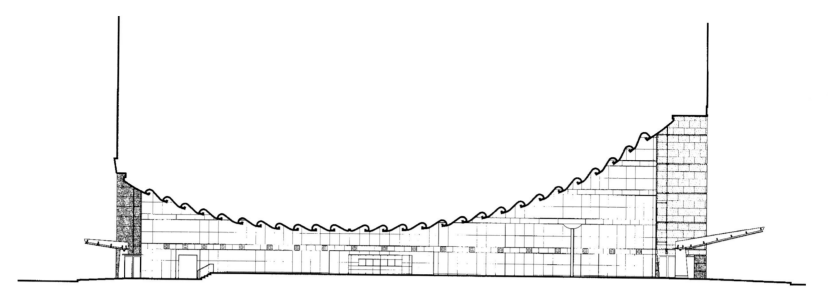

Top. Cross-section of the lobby on the ground floor that has been developed
at different heights, like a curved passage, crossing the elevator banks
to communicate the streets through the building. A false ceiling in the form
of an inverted parabolic dish covers the area accentuating the sensation
of depth along the route.
Bottom. Ground floor where the main lobby, three retail areas with independent
accesses from the street (Broadway), and a service area are found. There are
two accesses to the tower and the lobby crosses the lower floors of the building
connecting 42nd Street with 43rd Street.

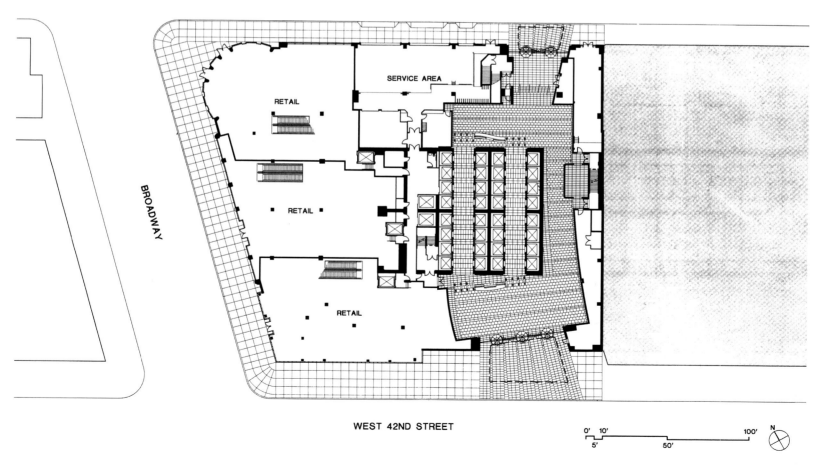

BROADWAY

SERVICE AREA

RETAIL

RETAIL

RETAIL

WEST 42ND STREET

Architect:

FOX & FOWLE ARCHITECTS P.C.

Developer:

Three Times Square Associates, LLC

Structural Engineering:

Severud Associates

Situation:

New York (New York, USA)

Project Date:

1999

Completion Date:

2001

Floors:

30

Height:

201 meters

Use:

Offices

Photography:

Andrew Gordon

The new corporate headquarters of Reuters American Holdings, the Reuters building, is also known as 3, Times Square and occupies a pivotal point in the heart of Manhattan. Situated in the central Times Square, it connects the commercial Seventh Avenue with the hectic 42nd Street celebrated for its theatrical environment and its leisure haunts. It faces the Condé Nast Building (work of the same architects and finalized in 1999) and forms part of the New York City Times Square revitalization project promoted by the City Hall, the Federal Government and private businesses to promote the urbanistic development of the center of Manhattan.

As far as urban scale is concerned, the building is a point where the energy of the city and the different existing volumes meet. The formal composition responds to the heterogeneity of its situation in such a way that each one of the facades has been given a specific treatment and volume. The building functions like a cubist picture. It offers multiple readings that unfold on each turn of 45 degrees.

Along 42nd Street, going north, we find the New Victory Theater building, which is not very high, and Times Square. The facade of the Reuters building responds with a seven-story podium made of terracotta and stone that reinterprets some of the motifs from the classical Times Square. The same thing happens with the remainder of the composition of the facade which is a square-grid of glass and stone. On reaching the corner, the base is maintained as an element that relates the building to a more urban and pedestrian scale. This rotates by means of a cylindrical figure and forms continuity with the glass curtainwall of the east facade.

Each one of the two corners is marked by its geometry and symbolism. The corner orientated to the south, cylindrical in form, is the one that has greater strength urbanistically. It is also where, in a more energetic form, the corporate image of Reuters is projected given that the corner is cov-

THE REUTERS

ered with video screens and luminous advertisements. Over the northwest corner, which is of more geometric lines, a luminous screen has been inserted on which the Reuters Index is broadcast. On the screen, the intensity and color of the words and letters vary according to the importance given to the news.

A reflection of what happens outside the building is transferred into the interior where the ground plan, again, is not homogeneous. Based on orthogonal figures, curved and irregular, the building sets textures, colors and styles against each other. Formally, it is organized around an interior communications nucleus leaving the remaining space to the perimeter free. This allows for irregular geometry in the floor plan and the introduction of different floor uses as neither the structure nor the nucleus vary. The formal synthesis of the more public lower floors contrasts with the remainder of the building that seeks a more regular geometry to take greater advantage of the interior space.

The final volume of the building contrasts with the classic skyscrapers of the first half of the 20th century and with those that were icons of the modern movement. As with all those good works of architecture, the Reuters Building expresses its time with diversity and responds to the consumer society, moral unrest and technological progress.

During the design process, the architects Robert F. Fox and Bruce S. Fowle invited developers and local authorities to actively participate in a search for solutions that would satisfy both public and private interests. The end result is the Reuters Building, a building that formed part of a municipal initiative to bring life to and rehabilitate the city center.

Frontal image of the south facade that stands out against the city's sky and delineates different forms. The outline of the building changes as it is viewed from the varying angles and heights of the different viewpoints from where it can be seen in the city.

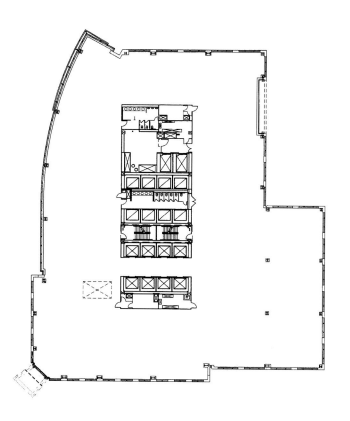

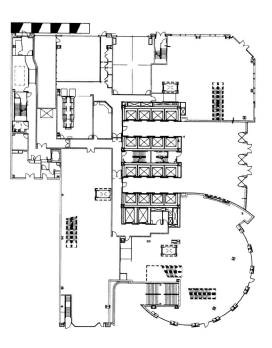

Top from left to right. Standard floor plan for the lower floors of offices and the ground floor itself. The distribution of the floors is organized around a central structural and communications nucleus. The ground floor has its main entrance from Seventh Avenue. On both sides of this entrance hall there are retail premises unique in their geometry. The building is situated in front of the Condé Nast Building (designed by the same architects) and close to the New Victory Theater and Times Square in 42nd Street.
Bottom from left to right. Elevation south, east, north and west.

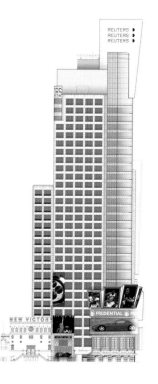
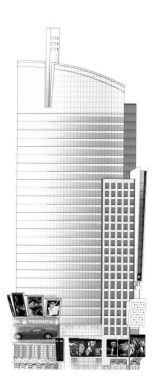
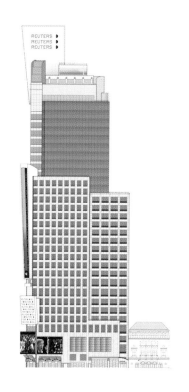
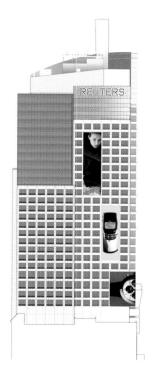

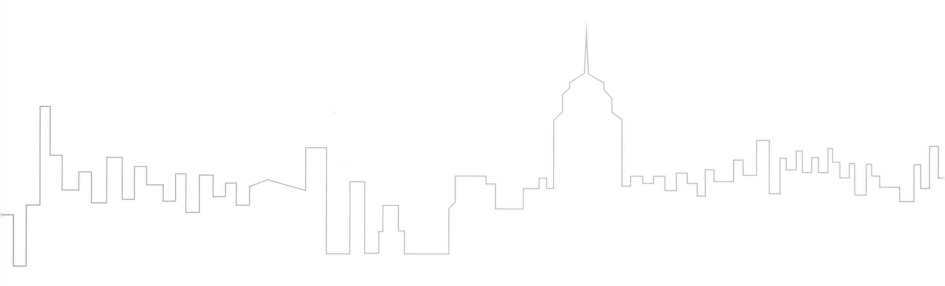

Born in Rome in 1944, he graduated as an architect in 1969 in La Sapienza (the faculty of architecture of the University of Rome). As a student, he combined his studies with working in the studios of the Italian artist Giorgio De Chirico and the Danish architect J Utzon in Copenhagen.

He established his own studio in 1970 in Rome and later in Paris (1989) and Vienna (1993). FUKSAS studios are multidisciplinary offices that count on a team formed by architects, urban developers, designers, landscapers and an important multimedia section which all together amounts to a total of 100 people (65 in Rome and 35 in Paris). For many years, the studio has dedicated special attention to the study of urban problems focusing on the outskirts of the city.

Massimiliano Fuksas has been a visiting lecturer in various universities of architecture such as Paris, Stuttgart, Wien and New York. He has obtained special mentions such as the Grand Prix d'Architecture Française and has won different prizes. Since January 2000, he publishes a weekly column on architecture in L'Espresso (founded by B Zevi).

1985	Sports Center, Paliano
1990	Cassino Town Hall
1991	Office Building for Edison Multimedia Activities, Saint-Quentin-en-Yvelines
1992	New Cemetery, Civita Castellana
1992	Maison des Arts, Exhibition Center, Multimedia Center, Workshops, Music Hall and Radio. University of Bordeaux
1995	Renovation: Place des Nations, Geneve
1997	Europark Shopping and Leisure Center, Salzburg
2001	Wien Twin Towers, Vienna
2002	Shopping and Leisure Center, Belpasso
2003	New offices for Ferrari S.p.A., Maranello

MASSIMILIANO FUKSAS
Studio Fuksas

MASSIM
FUKS

Architect:
MASSIMILIANO FUKSAS
Developers:
Immofianz Immobilien Anlagen AG,
Wienerberger Baustoffindustrie AG
Structural Engineering:
Büro Thumberger + Kressmeier, Viena
Situation:
Vienna (Austria)
Project Date:
1999
Completion Date:
2001
Floors
34 and 37
Height:
127 and 138 m
Use:
Offices and services
Photography:
Drexler
K. Furudate
Angelo Kaunat
Rupert Steiner

Massimiliano Fuksas is an architect who has become well known for giving special attention to the study of urban problems and, in particular, for the analysis of the structures of the suburbs. It was from this urban characteristic that the Twin Tower project took, as one of its starting points, the desire to find a solution that would form part of the city's outline. This is a city with a significant artistic tradition in which architecture holds a significant role. Vienna, as do other cities in central Europe, narrates part of the architectural history of the last few centuries: from the classicist buildings, through the Secession, and the interruption of the modern movement, to the present. Coop Himmelb(l)au headed the contemporary architectural debate with a constructive and critical spirit along with a social message. M. Fuksas found himself in a Vienna that was conservative, but, nevertheless, prepared to innovate.

The plot that was to receive the building was not within the consolidated weave of the city. From the beginnings of the assignment, the addition of a new area to the city was proposed. The new area was to bring forth new ideas to the model of urban growth and enrich the skyline with its presence as, with two towers of 34 and 37 floors, it would be an inevitable point of reference. Situated in a development zone between the density of built-up sectors and the open spaces of the outlying areas, these towers bring together and exalt the themes that have prevailed from their initial sketches. The creation of the new urban landscape in the Wienerberg, a recently created neighborhood in which mechanisms of self-identification should be apparent, presents this idea of the transition that is produced between the city and the country.

This process is transmitted in the public space, the south plaza, which has been created by the complex. Treated as a natural space, in a street that reminds us of winding rural roads, it has been designed (by the same architect) using concepts from Land Art. The approach and entrance be-

© Drexler

WIEN TWIN TOWER

© Angelo Kaunat

come an experience that introduces the spectator into the atmosphere of the building.

M. Fuksas's design proposes a new complex for mixed use based on two clearly differentiated volumes, "towers" and "bars", as two juxtaposed buildings. Distributing functions in independent elements allows for a clear and easy reading on the user's part: the leisure area is situated in the low building in contact with the public space and the office towers which, at a distance from the street, are connected one with the other by glazed walkways. The leisure-retail center consists of multi-screen cinemas, bars, restaurants and an underground car park with a capacity for 1,000 cars.

The functional organization of the tower responds to that of a central nucleus scheme that distributes the office spaces around the perimeter. The complete covering of the building is a totally transparent glass membrane that reveals its entrails to the city.

The Twin Towers exalt the themes presented in Maximiliano Fuksas's previous works: the development of the urban landscape, the connections and transitions between urban density and green spaces along with the complicity between art and architecture. The ethical aspects of the project on an urban scale lead to a re-reading of the infrastructures and privileges the accessibility and transparency of the new neighborhood.

© K. Furudate

© K. Furudate

Top. Detail of the facade. The building appears to be completely naked. The office furniture and the silhouettes of its occupants seem to float in space.
Bottom. Various views of the interior of the building that is characterized by the employment of translucent materials and glass in its outer casing which emphasizes the luminosity of its lobbies, entrances and transit areas.

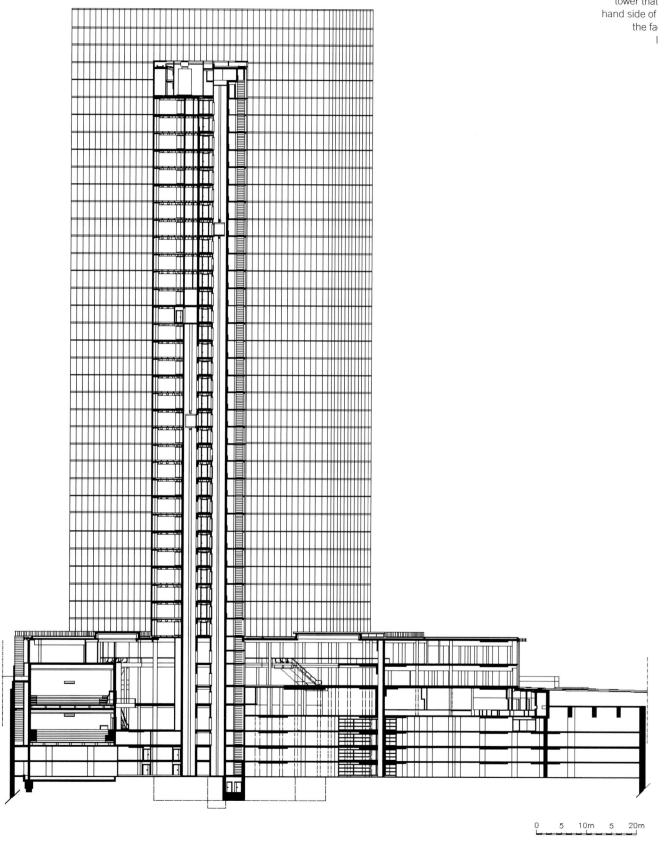

Cross-section of the vertical communications nucleus of tower B looking toward tower A. This is the tower that is situated on the right-hand side of the triangular base with the facade that gives onto the landscaped public area.

0   5   10m   5   20m

Top. Detail of the exterior of the facade and of the city that extends from the foot of the towers as if it were a carpet.
Bottom left: Sketch by M. Fuksas that illustrates his idea for the project: two glazed monoliths obliquely faced toward one another that establish numerous relationships.
Bottom center and right. Cross-section of tower A in which we can see how the two towers are linked by means of passageways various floors high as illustrated in the photograph that follows.

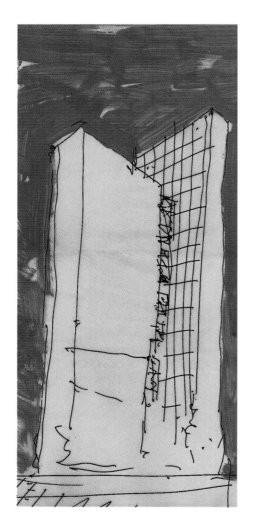

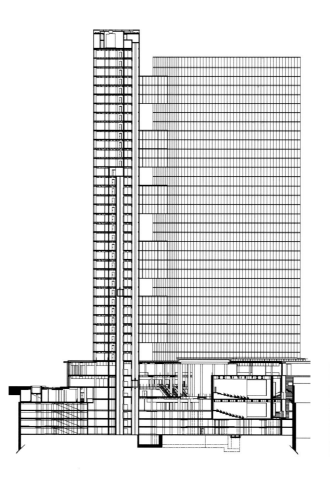

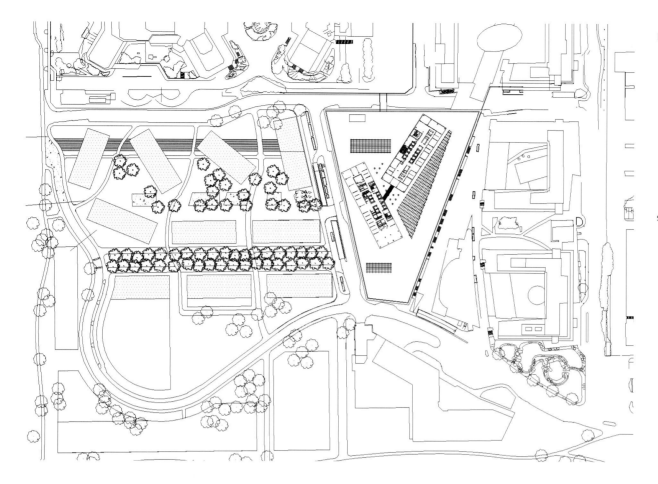

Top. Situation plan in which we can see the designs for the public space in front of the main entrance to the complex. The space has been dealt with as a non-urban landscape to which concepts of Land Art have been applied.

Bottom left. Ground floor of the leisure/retail center in which two pedestrian entrances and one vehicle entrance have been proposed; the stores, bars and restaurants have been distributed independently to create pathways and central spaces. Finally, a group of multi-screen cinemas delimits the western facade of the complex.

Bottom right. A plan of the roof of the complex that forms the base for the two towers. This area is used as a large terrace where bars, restaurants and three metallic pergolas are situated.

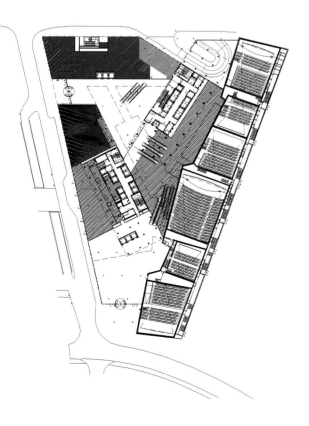

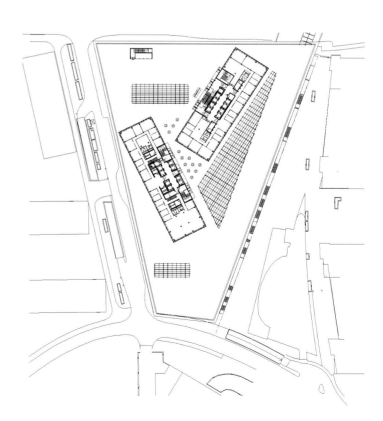

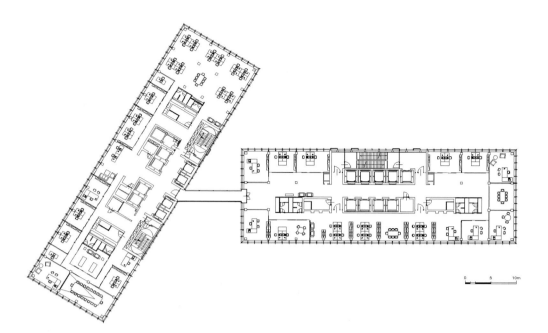

Top. A standard floor of the towers. Tower A (on the left) is placed diagonally, almost perpendicular, to tower B (on the right). The floor plan is T-shaped.
Bottom. Two exterior views of the complex: one from within the city and the other from an elevated angle that provides a more complete impression of the complex.

© Angelo Kaunat

© Angelo Kaunat

Top. Construction detail (elevated and section) of the glass facade. Bottom from left to right. Two aspects of the complex: an interior view and an exterior nocturnal view. The style based on the use of dark materials and discontinuous lighting in the leisure areas contrasts with the treatment of the entrances and lobbies that are characterized by their luminosity and translucent tones.

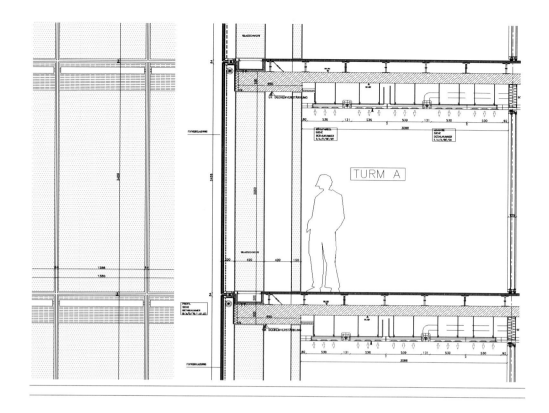

© Drexler

© Angelo Kaunat

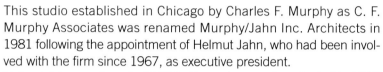

This studio established in Chicago by Charles F. Murphy as C. F. Murphy Associates was renamed Murphy/Jahn Inc. Architects in 1981 following the appointment of Helmut Jahn, who had been involved with the firm since 1967, as executive president.

Helmut Jahn was born in 1940 in Nuremberg and graduated in 1965 in the Technische Hochschule in Munich. In 1966, he left for the United States where he completed his studies in the Massachusetts Institute of Technology under the tuition of Mies van der Rohe.

During the 60's, the firm designed some of Chicago's most outstanding buildings using a vocabulary of Miesian geometry. The appearance of H. Jahn indicated a decisive break with the official ideology of the Modern Movement and led to the introduction of designs that were as rational as they were intuitive which account for the firm's international prominence.

The American Institute of Architects has declared that Helmut Jahn is one of the ten most influential living American architects. Murphy/Jahn's buildings have received numerous prizes and their designs and projects have been exhibited throughout the world.

www.murphyjahn.com

1974	Kemper Arena Stadium, Kansas City
1980	Xerox Center, Chicago
1985	James R. Thompson Center, Chicago
1986	One Liberty Place, Philadelphia
1991	Messeturm Tower, Frankfurt
1993	Hitachi Tower, Singapore
1998	Generale Bank Nederland, Rotterdam
1999	New European Union Headquarters, Brussels
2000	Sony Center, Berlin
2001	Shanghai International Expo Center (phase 1), Shanghai

HELMUT JHAN

Murphy/Jhan Inc. Architects

MURPHJHAN

Architect:

MURPHY/JAHN INC. ARCHITECTS

Developers:

Deutsche Grundbesitz Management (GmbH)

Structural Engineering:

Werner Sobek Ingenieure GmbH

Situation:

Frankfurt (Germany)

Project Date:

2000 (competition)

Floors:

63

Height:

228 meters

Use:

Offices, residential and retail

The building Max is to be situated in the financial center of Frankfurt (the City) where a forest of skyscrapers has been raised among the buildings of masonry that form the main substratum of the metropolis. Along side skyscrapers as emblematic as the Commerzbank (by the British architect Norman Foster) and others recently constructed such as the Rhein Main and Eurotheum towers 200 and 102 meters high respectively, the Murphy/Jahn project ventures to elaborate an individualistic image over which the surroundings should not become a conditioning factor. Jelmut Jahn proposes a slender volume of great density that would throw the shadow of an ellipse in an ascending movement.

This project won a competition for ideas for the construction of a new office building in an existing intermix, a traditional city block consisting of six-floor brick buildings along with a residential building of 24 floors in height, that is to be rehabilitated. The proposal fashions, in the lower floors, the different buildings that form part of the base of the tower and gives particular emphasis to the creation of a dynamic public space. This is to be achieved by mixing uses and pedestrian routes that cross the buildings at different points below the same paved area that unifies the space.

The extensive program for new offices (85,500 m²) generates a tower of a large volume, but, with the exception of the street level where the accesses for pedestrians and vehicles to the interior of the tower are located, does not admit the possibility for this to relate to the scale of the existing city. In contrast, it does, however, harmonize with the other city, that of the skyscrapers, which is growing rapidly in Frankfurt. From this perspective, it was decided to develop a building which would be distinguished by its persecution of gracefulness. Diverse strategies were used to arrive at the final solution that consists of emptying part of the constructed mass and in this way concentrating less material and greater transparency in the last floors.

MAX FRANKFURT

As the geometric center of the floor goes back, the building steps in on itself successively in four movements of eight levels (28 m) at a time and maintains a constant section until concluding the building in the last twenty-three stories. The floor plan (of an elliptical form) has been organized around a central service and communications nucleus and arranges the offices around its extensive perimeter which is free from corners and formal interruptions. An incision that runs tangent to the smaller arc of the ellipse marks an axis through which natural light penetrates into the interior where a small atrium is produced. The architects present this as "gardens in the heavens" that reinforce the strategy of making the building appear immaterial. During the night, the lighting enhances the silhouette of the tower and the play on open and closed forms.

The facade shows the complete process of how steel is gradually done away with and its surface area taken over by glass as the building soars toward the heights. At the same time, it redefines the nature of finishings for high buildings by proposing a skin that is not limited to being a mere covering that would oblige the installations to be complemented with mechanical air-conditioning systems to obtain the ideal degree of comfort for the user. In this way, the Max falls in with those contemporary proposals that work the facade as a complex mechanism with extended functions. It has also developed steel technology and, above all, it has established glass as being the material of contemporary architecture.

Project maquette and site plans
for the Max complex.
The 63-floor office tower
is the central axis of
this development project
for a complex of mixed uses.
It is to be situated on an existing
plot in the center of the city.

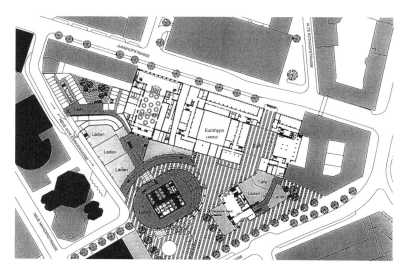

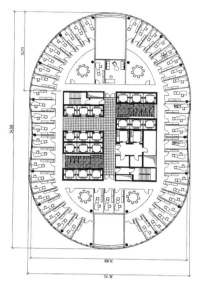 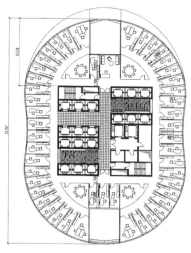 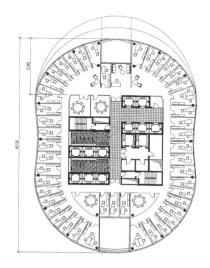 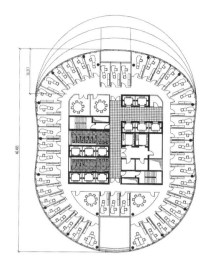

Top from left to right. Standard floors of the office tower that are distributed around a central nucleus.
Bottom left. North-west section of the site. The tower is found among historic elements of the city, which constitute the image of the block, a 24-floor residential building and the skyscrapers of the financial district.
Bottom right. Photomontage of the tower in its urban context side by side with the Commerzbank and the Rhein Main.

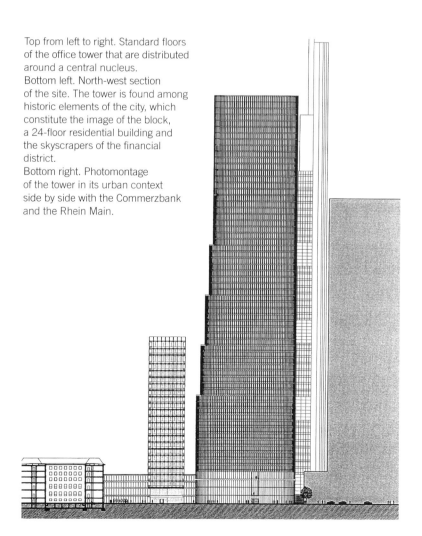

MURPH
JHAN

Architect:

MURPHY/JAHN INC. ARCHITECTS

Developer:

Sony Corporation Court

Structural Engineering:

Ove Arup & Partners, BGS,

Werner Sobek Engineers GmbH

Situation:

Berlin (Germany)

Project Date:

1993

Completion Date:

2000

Floors:

26

Height:

103 meters

Use:

Offices, residential and retail

Photography:

A.A. Garreta

Engelhardt / Stellin + Aschau i C.H.

H.G. Esch

John Linden

In 1991, a competition for ideas for the General Plan called Post-damer/Leipziger Platz was held. This marked the beginning of a process of urban renewal that preceded the demolition of the wall that divided the city of Berlin into two sectors. Situated on a triangular plot close to the Kulturforum area (where, among others, the Philarmonie and the Staatsbibliothek buildings by the architect Hans Scharoun and the National Galerie by Mies van der Rohe are found) the Sony Center was presented as a complex of multiuse buildings to herald the new millennium. The uses proposed include that of a cultural forum, a place to meet and for cultural and social exchanges, an activity center, residential zone and business center. From its construction to its installations, the building counts on the most advanced technology.

The volumetric considerations of the Sony Center have been determined by the General Plan: the buildings have been situated parallel to the main streets and organized in such a way that clearly reflects the desire that they should relate to their surroundings and echo the volumes and forms of nearby buildings. In the same way, the ruins of the famous Grand Hotel Esplanade, a luxury hotel of the early 20th century that lodged popular movie stars such as Greta Garbo and Charlie Chaplin, has been incorporated. The architect Helmut Jahn designed a sophisticated metallic structure that functions as a bridge and bears the weight of the new living spaces situated over the old structure of the hotel. He creates, in this way, an interesting juxtaposition of the old and the new.

The complex is structured in three elements: the Hochhaus postdamer Platz, the Sony headquarters (the only skyscraper within the complex) next to Sony and the Sony Forum. Within these, the Sony Plaza, a great oval central space covered by a large metallic dome that sifts light through canvases and which is surrounded by bars and restaurants, has been created. The user's experience is enriched through inhabiting dif-

Y

SONY CENTER

55

© H.G. Esch

fering spaces of varying qualities: open, covered and closed. The Sony Headquarters tower is an interesting variation of the classical skyscraper of mixed uses where functions are organized hierarchically in a vertical form: the retail areas are arranged on the lower floors and the residential on the upper levels. In this case, the different functions of the Sony Center extend horizontally with an arrangement of offices and living spaces in adjacent buildings that are open to the Sony Plaza and which support the structure of the oval metallic roof of the center.

The Sony Center, in short, presents itself as a virtual city within a city and, in fact, all of the new area Postdamer Platz has become the new center of Berlin taking the place of the old western center, the Berlin Mitte. In contrast with the treatment given to the Daimler complex (the urban development projected by the architect Renzo Piano, built and projected in the same period, which also forms part of the Postdamer Leipziger Platz) where the use of ceramics and opaqueness dominates the buildings, the Sony Center has a modern look created by glass and stainless steel which has been worked along with light (natural and artificial) as one of the essential elements of the design. Facades and roofs function as if they were transparent fabrics, porous, reflective and sophisticated that permit a constant succession of images as much during the day, as during the night.

© Engelhardt / Sellin + Aschau i C.H.

© A.A. Garreta

Top. Detail of the entrance hall to the tower of the Sony Center complex. The use of glass as a technical, structural and decorative material stands out.
Bottom from left to right. Detail of the ground floor and entrance. The structure of pillars that are situated behind the facade reaches the ground accompanied, in some sections, by the curtainwall which not only emphasizes the substantial curve of the facade, but also echoes the ground floor and creates a public porch.

Photographs of the great dome that covers the central plaza of the complex. The top photograph is an exterior shot taken from a height and the bottom one has been taken from within the plaza. The dome is situated at a great height and creates a space that is both interior and exterior. It is not a completely closed element, but open in the center. The dome also develops a mechanism for collecting rainwater by means of a structural element which conducts the collected water to a fountain.

© A.A. Garreta

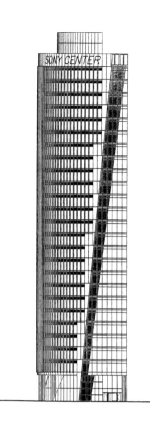

Top left. Detail of the fountain that is found in the center of the plaza set on a circular stainless steel platform and that has been divided into two equal parts. One part is at ground floor level while the other has been projected over the underlying floor.
Top right. Side elevation of the tower.
Bottom left. View of the central plaza through one of the accesses between two of the buildings by which it is formed.
Bottom right. The tower photographed from ground level with a detail of one of the sides which shows how the curtainwall has been treated as if it were a skin. Following page. Detail of the meeting point between the dome and one of the buildings that supports it.

© A.A. Garreta

© A.A. Garreta

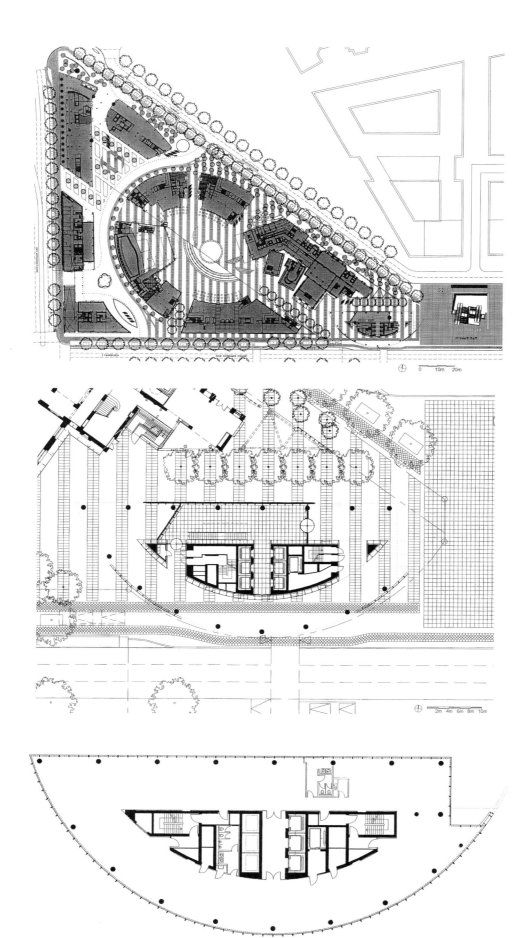

Situation plans for the Sony Center complex, which occupies a triangular plot on Postdamer Platz, the ground floor and a standard floor of the Sony Headquarters tower. The tower has been designed around a central structural and vertical communications nucleus in which the services have been situated. The cylindrical pillars that form the remainder of the structure have been positioned behind the plane of the facade.

Top left. Detail of the cladding for the facade and the curtainwall fixtures.
Top right. Exterior shot of the complex with the tower in the background.
Bottom left. Detail of the Esplanade Residence. This building conserves part of the old facade of the Great Hotel Esplanade and provides a historical reference for this part of the city. The new structure has been raised over the remainders of the hotel by means of a sophisticated structural system.
Bottom right. Detail of the curtainwall that forms the facade of the tower in which we can see the openings that form the natural ventilation system.

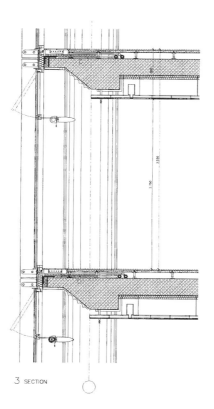

3 SECTION

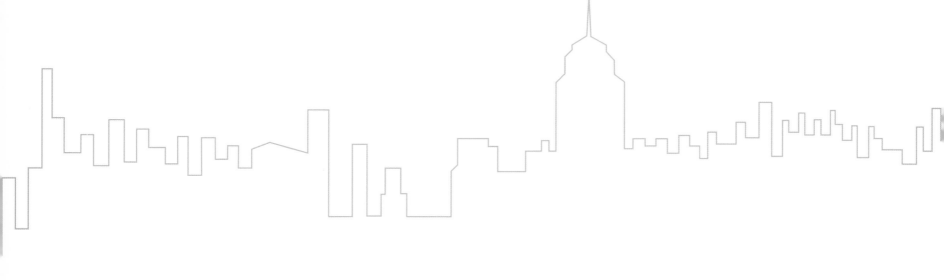

KPF was founded by Eugene Kohn, William Pedersen and Sheldon Fox in 1976 in New York. Since then, they have designed a large number of different types of buildings: museums, hotels, institutional buildings, retail centers and buildings related to education, leisure and transportation. C. Norberg-Schultz has emphasized KPF's intense work in the development of proposals for high buildings or skyscrapers and particularly the role of William Pedersen who has designed such emblematic buildings as 333 Wacker Drive (Chicago, 1984) and the DG Bank Headquarters (Frankfurt, 1995).
William Pedersen graduated in 1961 in the University of Minnesota and in 1963, he took his doctor's degree in the Massachusetts Institute of Technology. In addition, he has received numerous national and international prizes and is a member of various professional and institutional associations.
In their architecture, we discover a desire to design buildings which refer to the past, but that, at the same time, reflect the present and the future. Buildings that combine the formal with the informal simultaneously, the figurative with the abstract, the monumental with the humane and the modern with tradition.

www.kpf.com

1979	WABC-TV Studios, New York
1983	333 Wacker Drive, Chicago
1989	900 North Michigan Avenue, Chicago
1992	Federal Reserve Bank of Dallas, Dallas
1998	Samsung Plaza & Rodin Museum, Seoul
2000	JR Central Towers, Nagoya
2001	Plaza 66, Shanghai
2001	Brauch College Academic Complex, New York
2001	5 Times Square, New York
2003	Taichung Tower II, Taichung

A. EUGENE KOHN, WILLIAM PEDERSEN

Kohn Pedersen Fox Associates P.C.

KHON
PEDEF

Architect:

KOHN PEDERSEN FOX ASSOCIATES PC

Developer:
Hang Lung Development Co.Ltd.

Structural Engineer:
Thornton-Tomaseti Engineers

Situation:
Shanghai (The People's Republic of China)

Project Date:
1994

Completion Date:
2001 (Phase I)

Floors:
60

Height:
281 meters

Use:
Offices, residential and retail

The complex Plaza 66, popularly known as Nanjing Xi Lu, is situated along the most commercial street of the center of Shanghai. As has happened with many of the skyscrapers built in the Asian continent over the last few years, the impact generated in the traditional city will condition its future development. Plaza 66 will become one of Asia's most important cultural and financial centers in the coming years.

One of the starting points for the assignment was to transfer urban scale to the building and its immediate surroundings. The final solution is the result of mixing a series of volumes (a parallelepiped, a cone, an almond-shaped form and an arc) to form a collage. Each volume is distinguished for its own particular section and geometry. The resulting forms lead to an architectural exuberance that reflects the vibrant life in the street Nanjing Xi Lu.

With a plan for mixed uses, the complex is organized from a five-floor retail building. This ties in with the traditional profile of the city and, situated along the street, is interrupted by two office towers that are respectively 47 and 66 floors high. This podium is a purely visual element. It is not the substructure of the towers and, in fact, it only intersects with the highest. The subsequent vision of the complex reflects and emphasizes the independence of each building although the idea of forming a group has not been lost, as can be observed in details such as the covered pedestrian walkway that communicates the two towers.

The whole development plays with the idea of collage so that the retail building is not a unique piece, but responds to the juxtaposition of various curve-shaped volumes. Formally, it is a closed building that allows two glass figures placed at each extreme to appear. They are spaces open to the exterior that flood the street with light like a lamp during the night. They are large halls where galleries, ramps and stairs are situated along the facades. They are interior plazas that attract and invite the passer-by to visit the building.

PLAZA 66

From a structural point of view, Plaza 66 works in a way that is currently standard for a building of this type. The structure is distributed between the facade and a central nucleus where the vertical communications and some other services are concentrated. With an independent access for each of the buildings on the ground floor, which separates the main functions of the complex, the global design responds to a desire to create a group with a harmonic composition. The facades of the towers are made of aluminum and glass and flank the curved base of the retail area. The use of hard stone on the lower floors gives the building the necessary solidity to establish a counterweight with the height of the towers. Both of which are topped with an undulating screen and a light that emits subtle flashes during the night.

A distinctive aspect that draws attention to Plaza 66 is the use of a formal language that manages to evade conventional forms. To sum up, it deals with the functional and urbanistic demands of a high building by using diagonals, curves, undulations and so on which is not very common in the architecture of skyscrapers.

Top. Nocturnal view of the retail block formed by various volumes.
Bottom left. Detail of one of the ground floor entrances. The materials that predominate in the building are stainless steel and glass.
Bottom right. Plaza 66 as seen from the street Nan Jing Xi Lu in a nocturnal image in which the tower stands out along with the base, the latter, mainly due to the illumination.

Photographs of a fragment of the leisure and retail center situated on the ground floor and that, being between five and six floors in height, takes on the scale of a more traditional city. The retail block is interrupted by the two large glass volumes that break the continuity of its vertical cladding.

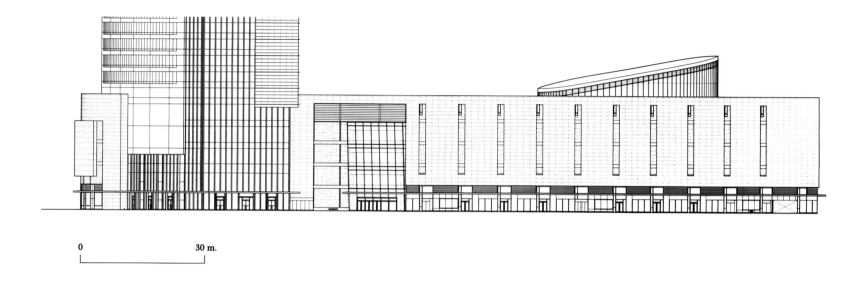

Top. North elevation of the base of the towers that forms the leisure and retail complex of Plaza 66.
Bottom left. Photograph of the scale model in which the complete complex is shown.
Bottom right. North elevation of the Plaza 66 complex that corresponds to the photograph of the scale model.

0   30 m.

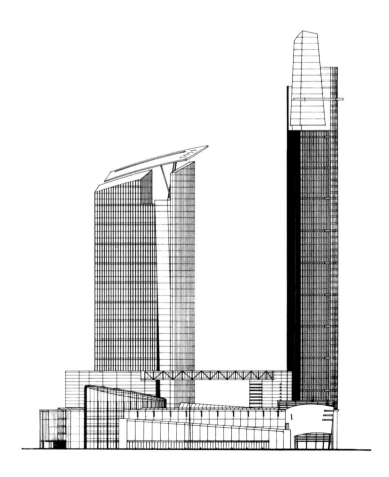

Bottom left. Photograph of the scale model. The two towers are balanced over the walkway which connects them in such a way that neither of the towers ever completely hinders the user's vision.

Bottom right. Elevation of the highest of the two towers (60 floors) and the first to be completed. Made of glass and granite, its composition based on horizontal trimmings is crowned by a glazed element that characterizes it in the city's skyline.

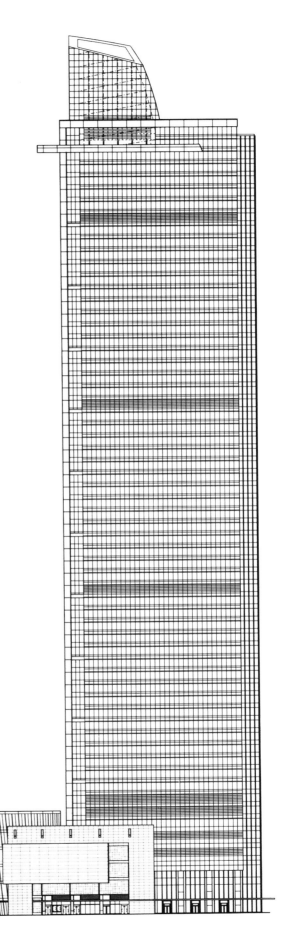

Top left. Interior image of the retail center as seen in the scale model for the project.
Bottom. One of the entrances to the office tower.

Right. Situation plan for the Plaza 66 complex that occupies a complete block in the center of the City of Shanghai. The main pedestrian entrance is situated in the Avenue Nan Jing Xi Lu. Vehicle access is available from the surrounding streets and leads to parking lots both underground and on the surface.

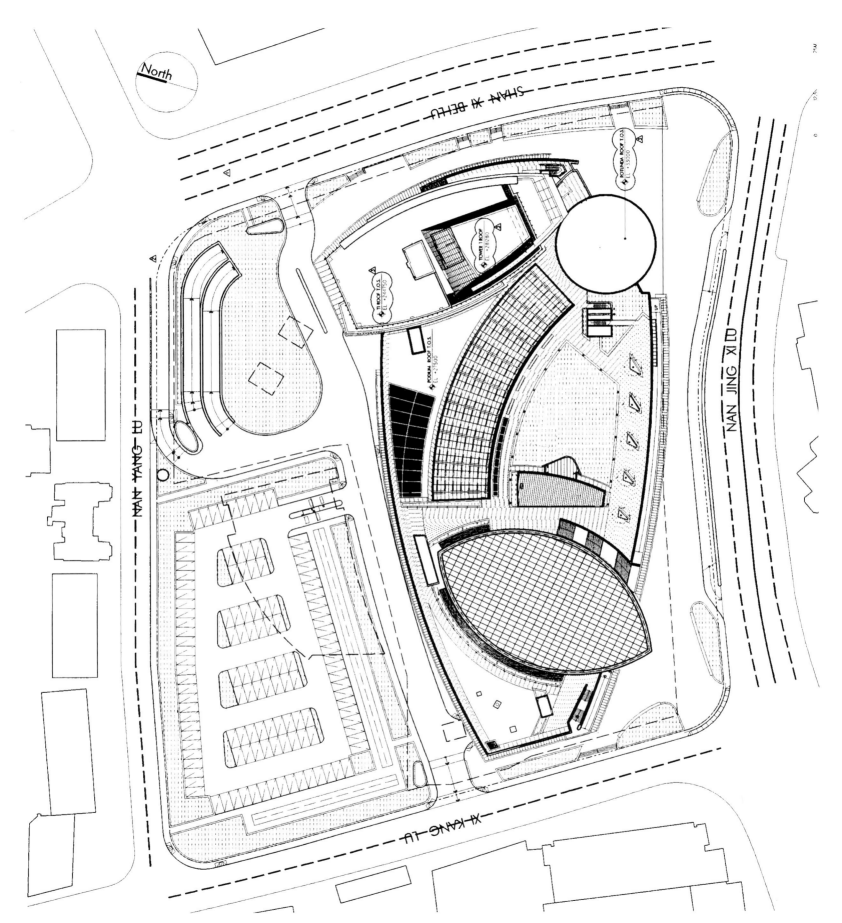

North

SHAN XI BEI LU

NAN JING XI LU

NAN YANG LU

XI KANG LU

ROTUNDA ROOF T.O.S.
EL +33000

TOWER 1 ROOF
EL +28080

T1 ROOF T.O.S.
EL +244750

PODIUM ROOF T.O.S.
EL +27500

Architect:
KOHN PEDERSEN FOX ASSOCIATES PC

Developer:
JR Tokai

Structural Engineering:
Taisei Corporation

Situation:
Nagoya (Japan)

Project Date:
1990

Completion Date:
1999

Floors:
59

Height:
250 meters

Use:
Hotel, offices, retail and services

The JR Central Towers complex is situated in Nagoya, the third largest metropolis in Japan. The challenge presented by the assignment consisted of integrating a mixed scheme of uses such as stores, a hotel, a cultural center, offices and parking lot with a major station through which the high velocity bullet train (the Shinkansen), the subway and various buses circulate. In addition, it was to be prepared to receive the future magnetic train. The project was developed jointly with Japan Central Railways and the Tokyo based architectural studio, Sakakura Associates.

The complex is located on a significant site at the entrance to the city among traditional urban intermix and, due to its employment of high technology, exterior image and diversity within its functional scheme, is a door to the 21st century. Over a 20-floor-high podium, two towers have been raised. Their connection with the horizontality of the podium provides a link with the present context; their height anticipates the buildings that will inevitably be raised within a few years.

The two towers have different forms and uses. However, they share a uniform exterior treatment that harmonizes with that of the totality of the complex. The highest tower is destined to offices and its geometry is the result of a square intersected by a cylinder. The ground floor concentrates the vertical communications as a central nucleus and frees the remainder of the tower. A hotel with 800 rooms occupies the second tower which is cylindrical and lower in terms of height. Both facades are continuous, free of corners, highly functional and neutral. The verticality of the stainless steel uprights over the glass that has also been cut into vertical strips dominates.

The bulk of the scheme is concentrated in the podium. This is a rectangular building of great complexity as it houses the confluence of the structures and vertical communications nuclei (elevators and stairs) of the two

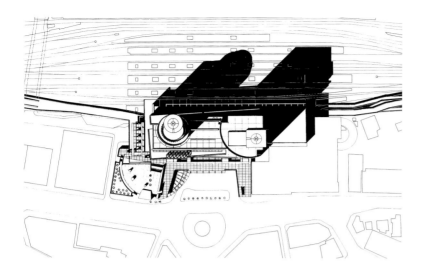

Top. Situation plan of this large complex that includes, among other facilities, an intermodal station.
Bottom left and right. Views of the facade of the rectangular building that forms the 20-floor base for the two towers. The three elements as seen from the street.

towers along with each of their own nuclei and structure. It is an intermodal building which is accessed on foot or by car from a large plaza where there are two exterior ramps leading to underground parking lots that are found in the same building. Access to the subway and train platforms is also available from the plaza.

The main lobby on the ground floor is a large interior public space. It connects with the large commercial center (that occupies more than half of the total surface of the building), with two floors dedicated to cultural activities, with the office tower parking lot (that occupies a third of the building), with the vestibules of both towers and with a transit area that the architects have called "Sky Street". This space, two floors high with a glass roof, functions as an interior street and this is where the majority of the building's movement is concentrated. Exteriorly, it seems to be an exempt volume that emphasizes the horizontal character of the building's facade which is only interrupted by a vertical element that ties in with the towers that have been set back into a secondary plane. The exterior design of the complex responds to a desire to create a composition which is harmonic, sculptural and dynamic and which explains the transference from the traditional city to the contemporary metropolis.

Top. Ground floor of the building that forms the base for the two towers and floor plan of the lower levels where most of the public activities are concentrated.
Bottom. Standard floor plan of the cylindrical tower which is used as a hotel.

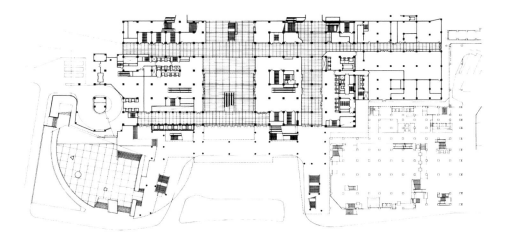

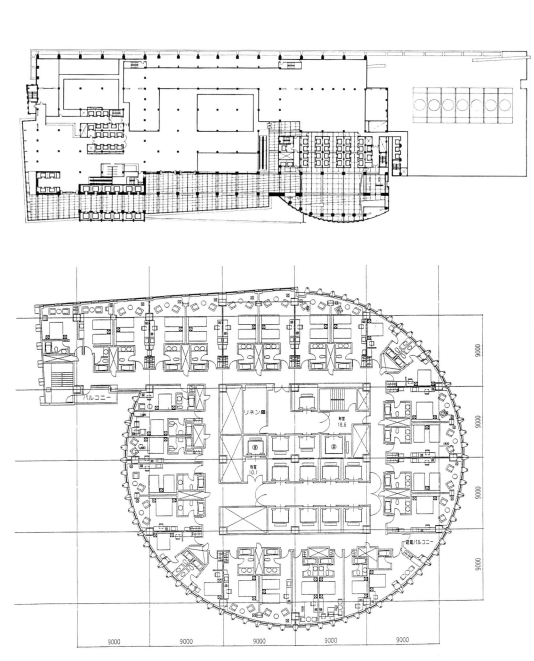

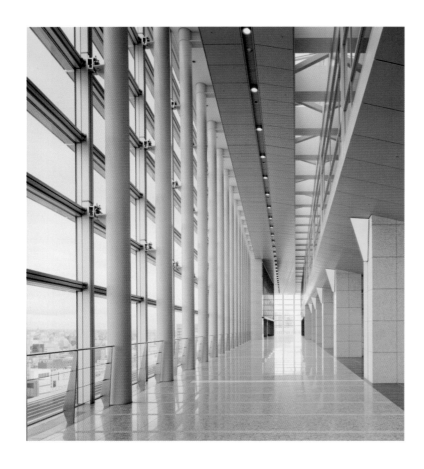

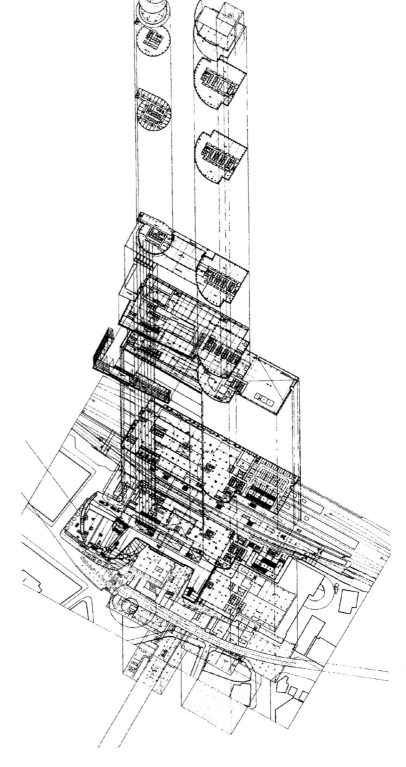

Photograph of one of the pedestrian
transit areas from the rectangular
building. In this project, it was very
important to analyze the users'
necessities to create a satisfactory
circulation system.
Bottom. An axonometric drawing of
the entire complex from the ground
floor to the top of the towers.

Section of the complex in which areas have been colored according to their uses: the 53-floor tower on the left accommodates the hotel; the 51-floor tower on the right, the offices; most of the base of the towers is destined to a retail center; and one third of the building is a 17-story parking lot. In addition, the two floors colored in yellow are dedicated to leisure and cultural activities.

Bottom. Nocturnal view of the main facade of the complex which, due to the circular form of its base and the two towers, gives the impression of being a gateway to the Nagoya of the 21st Century.

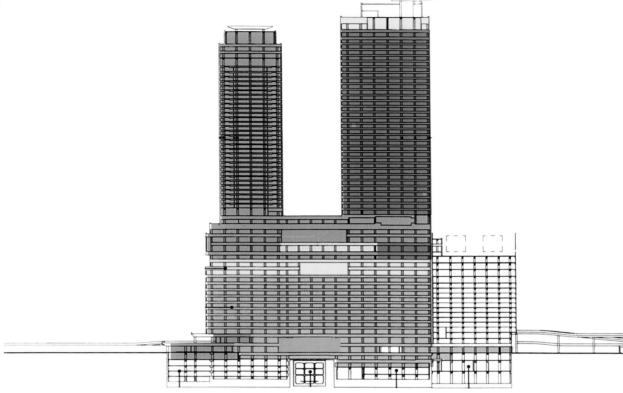

Architect:

KOHN PEDERSEN FOX ASSOCIATES PC

Developer:

Tzung Tang Development Co.Ltd.

Structural Engineering:

Weiskpf & Pickworth Consulting Engineers

Situation:

Taichung (Taiwan)

Project Date:

1996

Completion Date:

2003

Floors:

47

Height:

176 meters

Use:

Offices and hotel

The tower Taichung II is a building for mixed uses that offers office space and accommodates a 300 room hotel. Its exterior image is neutral and compact and defined by an elegant curtainwall made of glass, metal and stone which opens toward a large park and is opposite the city center. The design of the building has been inspired in the symbolism of Chinese culture. The form of the floor plan evokes that of a fish oriented to the east, a symbol of good fortune.

The spatial distribution of the ground floor should permit the coexistence of the functional schemes. On the one hand, the hotel requires a number of facilities and services given that each room is to have a bathroom and on the other, the floors dedicated to offices require as much space as possible so as to be able to accommodate the maximum amount of working areas. The metallic structure works basically with pillars placed following a number of porches in a perpendicular direction to the southern and northern facades. These should allow for the distribution of stair and elevator wells. The oval form of the floor plan and the fact that it is open toward the east allows, in the office levels, for the major part of the vertical communications nuclei and services to be concentrated in this direction. In this way, it leaves the remainder of the space from where there are views of the park free and minimizes, at the same time, the strong radiation of the afternoon sun.

The structural system was calculated to withstand the earthquakes of great intensity that are common in Taiwan. In the year 1999, while the tower was under construction, it successfully passed its first test. It should be borne in mind that the form of the building endures the horizontal forces best in an east-west direction. Therefore, the final form partly conditioned the election of the structural arrangements.

The form of the floor plan opens toward the east and closes toward the

Bottom left. Digital perspective of the building that has been raised as a prismatic volume over a north to south orientation. The lateral facades tend to function as wings that free the outer casing from the facade into two slightly curved planes.
Bottom right. Longitudinal section of the central nucleus of the tower from east to west.

west leading to two of the freestanding tower's four facades practically disappearing. The favorable orientation, north-south, makes the most of the environmental factors and the occurrence of solar radiation in the interior of the building. The structure forms a corset that sustains the facade. This is formed by two glazed planes that smoothly curve and are raised over a base of pillars on the ground floor. The surface area of each level of the building is reduced with elevation. As a result of this, the curtainwall of the facade curves inwards and gives the building great poetic simplicity. On the roof, a lightly ovoid cylinder tops the building that, along with the continuous treatment of the top floor of the facade plane, identify the tower in the city's skyline.

The base, on the ground floor, is formed by a portico of pillars which are covered, in contrast to the other floors, with hard stone. On this level, as it is in contact with the street, the hotel's installations for public functions are situated. Also the differentiated treatment of the building's shaft and smaller scale is directed to the local urban context. On the ground floor, the building generates a large public space. This is a landscaped plaza which has been designed under the influence of the tower and integrates the space into the large adjacent park. The pure and beautiful form of the building makes it recognizable from any point of the city which transforms it into a symbol that, at night, is illuminated.

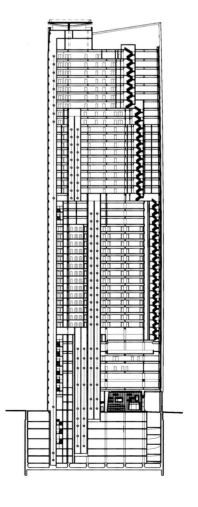

Top left. Side elevation that shows the ascending movement experienced by the volume of the tower and that emphasizes, in this way, the slenderness of its form.
Top right. Digital perspective of the interior of the building.
Bottom. Two exterior images that clearly show the volume of the tower.

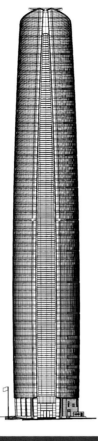

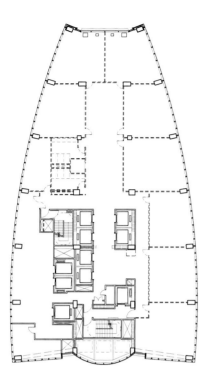
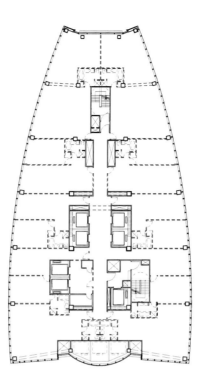
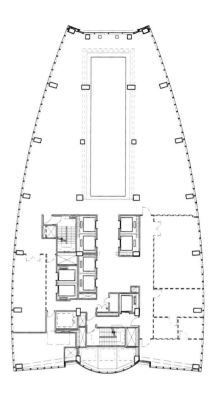

Top from left to right. Standard floor plans of the tower from the lower levels, which are mainly dedicated to public functions, to the higher ones, which combine a hotel and offices. The building is crowned by a cylindrical glazed element in which an exclusive club for executives with privileged views of the city is located.

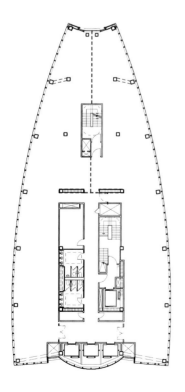
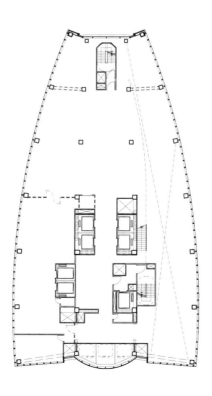
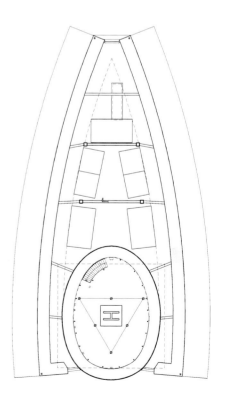

Top. South elevation of the tower and
north-south section.
Bottom. Two images of the building
during the period of its construction
in which the metallic structure
is uncovered and appears as if
it were a skeleton. It will be covered
with a curtainwall of glass, metal
and stone slabs.

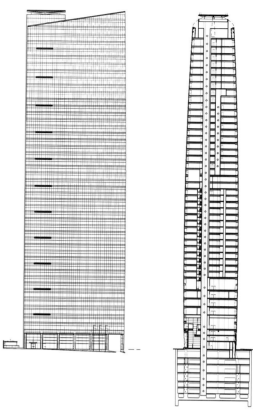

Established in Hong Kong in 1994, the firm Dennis Lau & Ng Chun Man has its origins in the firm Ng Chun Man & Associates that was created in 1974. This studio, with a staff of more than 300, develops projects that include architecture, urban development, interior design and landscaping.

They are currently working in a large number of countries in the southeast of Asia including, for example, Singapore and Taiwan. Another of the countries where their work is clearly visible is China where, at present, there are more than 30,000 architects. Because of this, a presence in this country is indispensable given the existence of such competition, dependence and rivalry among the architectural studios in Hong Kong that, as recognized by Dennis Lau himself, will increase in the future.

www.dln.com.hk

1986	Hong Kong University, Hong Kong
1989	Park Towers Complex, Hong Kong
1989	University Residence YWCA, Hong Kong
1991	Golden Center, Hong Kong
1992	Central Plaza, Hong Kong
1994	Lee Theatre Plaza, Hong Kong
1995	Citic Plaza, Guanghou
1996	Lee Gardens, Hong Kong
1997	The Commissioner's Building, Hong Kong
1998	The Center, Hong Kong

DENNIS LAU
Dennis Lau & NG Chun Man,
Architects & Engineers

DENNIS
NG CHUN

Architect:

DENNIS LAU & NG CHUN MAN ARCHITECTS + ENGINEERS (H.K.) LTD

Developer:

Urban Renewal Authority & Cheung Kong Ltd

Structural Engineering:

Maunsell Consultant Asia Ltd

Situation:

Hong Kong (The People's Republic of China)

Project Date:

1995

Completion Date:

1998

Floors:

78

Height:

346 meters

Use:

Offices

The completion of this building, currently the third highest skyscraper in Hong Kong, confirms that the construction boom in this city has continued although British rule has ended. While the expansion in construction that thrived between 1970 and 1980 was concentrated in new cities of the interior, the skyscrapers of the 90's were built in the congested center of Hong Kong which has brought about a considerable increase in the height of the city's skyline.

The local architectural studio Dennis Lau & Ng Chun Man has responded to this boom, which has converted the center of the city into a forest of concrete towers, by raising the elegant building The Center. Situated in a dynamic business neighborhood, it stands out for the attractive exterior aspect it offers. Its design responds to the needs of pedestrians and of the users of the office spaces. Also, given that land is scarce on the island, the use of each square meter of the floor plan has been maximized to maintain low costs.

The Center is well known for being an intelligent building from a technological point of view. This has been achieved by the incorporation of domotics to control, by means of a computer, aspects such as exterior and interior lighting, heating, air conditioning and security systems. It was the first building in the city to incorporate an automatic hanging basket for the maintenance and cleaning of the facades.

346m in height, including the antenna that tops the building, it has become an identifiable silhouette within the city's skyline. The restrained reflective glass curtainwall of the facade along with the spectacular nocturnal lighting make it stand out from the mass of buildings that surround it.

Formally, the building presents very pure volumes that are accentuated by the regularity in treatment given to the curtainwall which is completely glazed (neither fittings nor fixings are visible). The only exceptions to this are where the building meets the ground, to allow for access, and the topping. The star-shaped polygon design of the floor plan is the result of the superimposition and rotation by 45° of two identical squares. The communications nuclei are concentrated in the center in the form of a cross that frees the

THE CENTER

remainder of the space to permit maximum optimization in distribution. The seventy-three floors of offices have been raised over a large atrium decorated in granite, glass, vegetation and water. This fifteen-meter-high space also includes a retail area. Access from outside is available through a cylindrical shaft after a stroll through a garden which has been incorporated into the interior of the building. By this gesture, the architect, Dennis Lau, has introduced a space that functions as a place of rest, a place that provides an interval between the chaotic traffic and the frantic activity of the financial district.

The building is classical in the sense that its inspiration lies in the purest tradition of the American skyscrapers of the 30's and 40's. This is, however, a reading that is infrequently found in this continent where buildings of this type generally illustrate the technological culture.

Top. Detail of how one of the sides of the octagon projects over the ground floor.
Bottom left. Detail of the main entrance that shows the characteristic use of natural materials (in this case granite) and stainless steel.
Bottom right. View of one of the corners of the tower from street level. The cladding finishes upon arriving at ground floor level so that only the structure reaches as far as the street and extends toward the subsoil. The openness of the constructed mass gives rise to a large public space.

Top and bottom. Details of the ground floor and the public space in which the incorporation of different forms of vegetation (such as bamboo which is so characteristic of the Asian continent) along with aquatic areas help to create a relaxing atmosphere that distances momentarily (the time the short stroll from the street to the interior of the building lasts) the noise from the street.

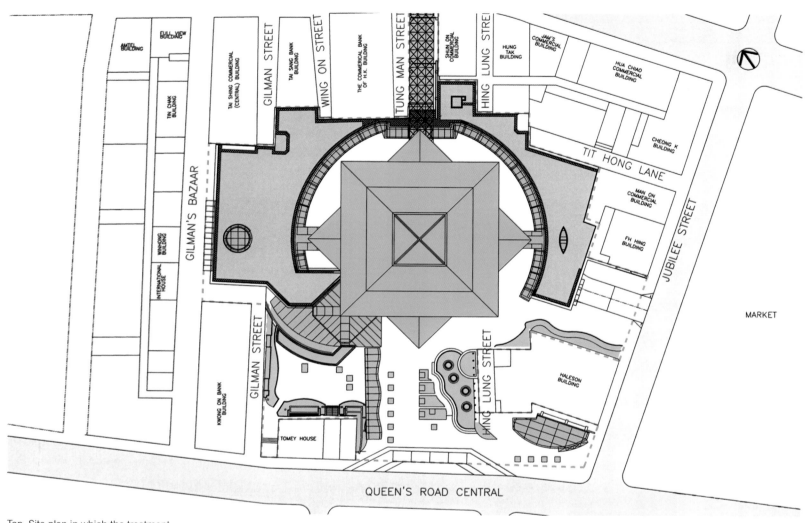

Top. Site plan in which the treatment of the public space in front of the main entrance can be seen. The undulating forms break with the building's geometry. Bottom. Standard floor plan of the tower that has been formed by superimposing one square rotated by 45 degrees over another. An octagonal form is created which allows for the distribution of offices around a central nucleus.

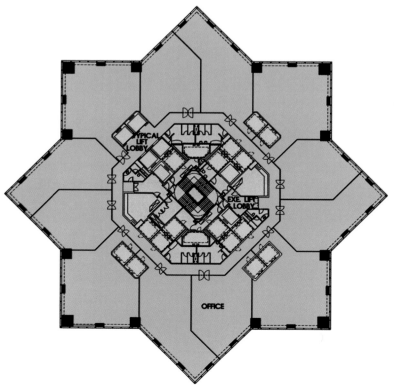

Top. Detail of one of the corners
of the tower at its meeting point
with the ground floor. The tower is
characterized by its purity in line,
its changes in plane and the images
that are reflected in its facades.
Bottom left. Elevation and section of
the building that reveals its formal
construction, from its starting point on
the ground floor to the classical
gesture by which it is topped.
Bottom right. A shot of the building
from the plaza which lies between
the main entrance to the building
and Queen's Road Central

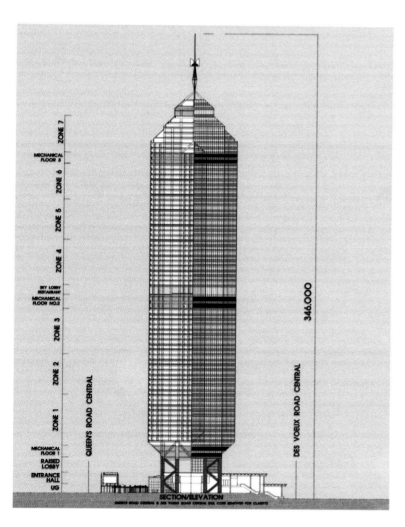

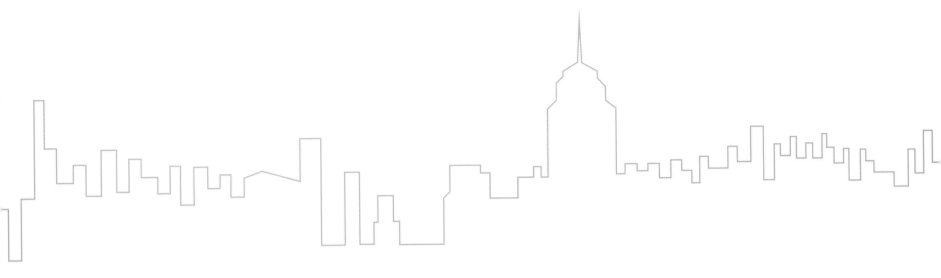

Enric Miralles (Barcelona 1955-2000), after Gaudí, was the most fundamental Catalan architect of 20th century architecture. He graduated in 1978 in architecture in l'Escola Tècnica Superior d'Arquitectura de Barcelona university in which he was a regular teacher from 1985 and professor from 1996. His educational activity along with his great capacity to communicate took him to collaborate with other American and European universities. The Col.legi d'Arquitectes de Catalunya awarded him their gold medal in July 2002.

Benedetta Tagliabue was born in Milán and graduated as an architect in 1989 in the Instituto Universitario d'Architettura di Venezia. She began to collaborate with Miralles in 1990 in Barcelona and in 1993, they formed the studio Enric Miralles - Benedetta Tagliabue Arquitectes Associats that she currently directs.

Among the projects currently being undertaken by the studio are The Scottish Parliament in Edinburgh, Scotland, the School of Architecture in Venice (IUAV), Santa Caterina Market and the new headquarters for Gas Natural which are both in Barcelona.

www.mirallestagliabue.com

1985	Roofs in Parets del Vallès (Barcelona)
1990	Olympic Games Archery Installations, Barcelona
1993	Hostalets de Balenyà Social Center (Barcelona)
1994	Home-School, Morella
1995	Heaven Pavilion for the Tateyama Museum, Tateyama
1995	Igualada Cementary Park (Barcelona)
2000	Music School, Hamburg
2000	Utrecht City Hall, Utrecht
2001	Mollet del Vallès Park and Civic Center (Barcelona)
2002	Diagonal Mar Park, Barcelona

ENRIC MIRALLES, BENEDETTA TAGLIABUE
E.M.B.T. Arquitectes Associats

Architect:

ENRIC MIRALLES & BENEDETTA TAGLIABUE ARQUITECTES ASSOCIATS

Structural Engineering:

Gas Natural SDG

Ingeniero de Estructuras:

MC2 Estudio de Ingeniería

Situation:

Barcelona (Catalonia, Spain)

Project Date:

1999

Completion Date:

2004

Floors:

21

Height:

86 meters

Use:

Offices

Photography:

Lourdes Jansana

This office block that will be (in its highest part) the central headquarters of the Barcelona company Gas Natural (formerly known as Catalana de Gas) will be bordered by a by-pass (el Cinturó del Litoral) near the Olympic Village, the new Diagonal Mar Park (by the same architects) and the popular Barceloneta quarter (the city's old fishing district) which is made up of small dwellings along side the old gasometers which maintain the memory of both the city and company's industrial past. This is a special place where different urban fabrics that are full of their own energies intermix. From here, views of the sea and of almost the entire city will be available.

The architects' desire while developing this new tower was to make it compatible with the immediate urban surroundings - this is one of the essential problems with high-rise buildings – by understanding the surroundings and making the building conform to all the strengths that flow within them. It expresses a will to enter into the debate on how the city should grow and about how a particular quarter can absorb transformations in its infrastructures and at the same time enable the local population to adapt to the new situation. The building responds with the verticality of a tower while, at the same time, it fragments itself into smaller elements that give rise to a 35m corbel that forms a unique public space within an urban landscape with differing dimensions. This space becomes a large gateway to Barceloneta, the adjacent neighborhood.

The design has been based on a human scale and tries to deal with the building-city-person relationship as a working tool by using metaphors that transform a vertical building into one that is horizontal.

Maybe, the most important aspect of the building is that we will be able to enter a space previously defined as private. This space will now be public and the old park and gasometers have been adapted to provide one of its most important accesses.

GAS NATURAL

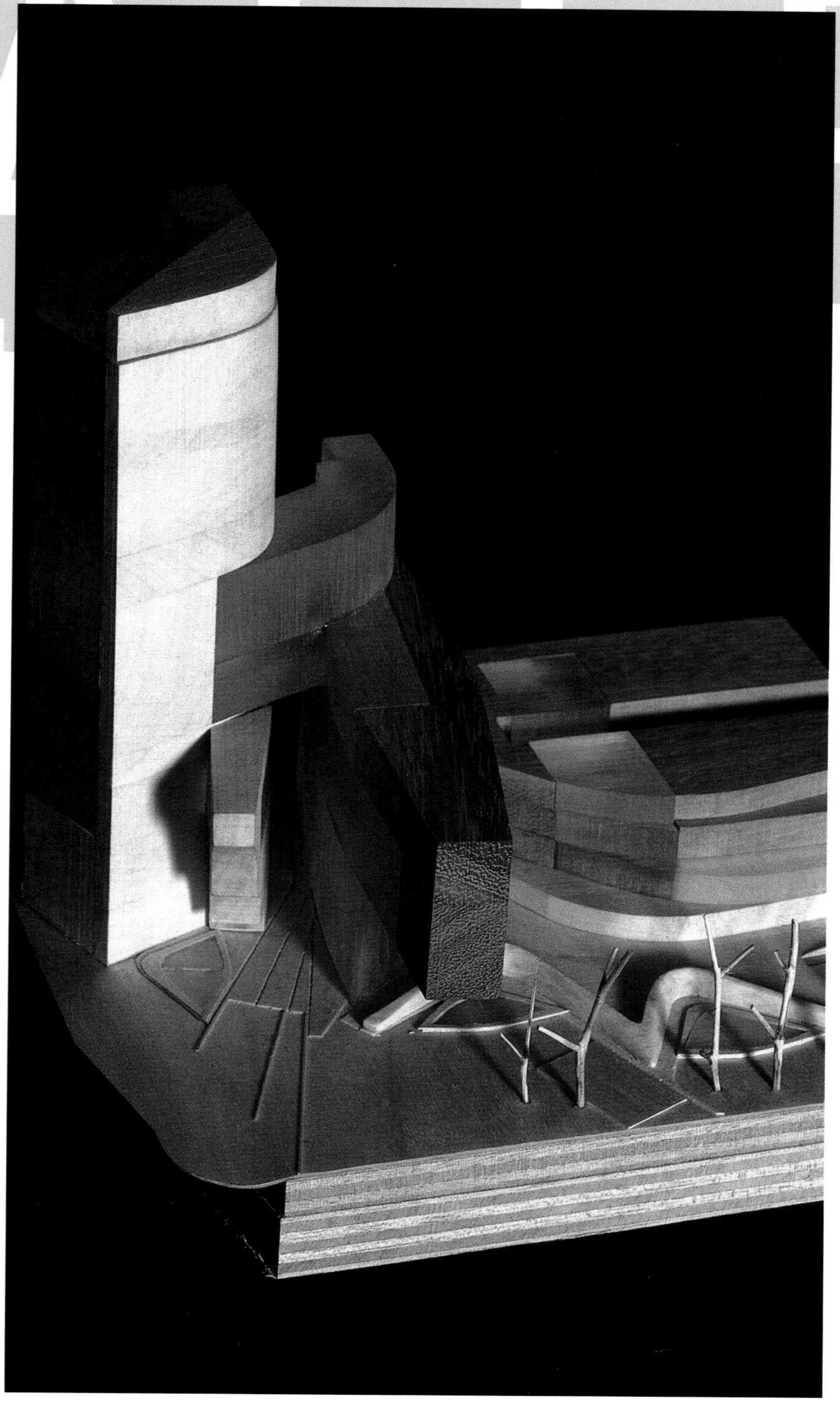

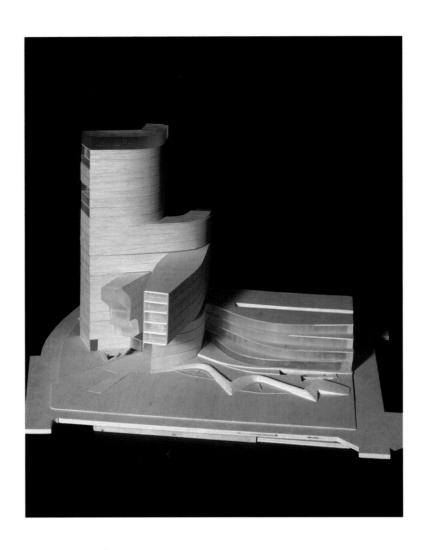

From its proposed uses, from the most private to the most public, we can clearly see the functions that it is to fulfill: twenty floors dedicated to offices; three to parking (the first one partially destined to loading and unloading); an auditorium with 100 seats in the first basement; an exhibition area on a mezzanine floor; a cafeteria on the ground floor oriented toward the interior garden; and a public street in the interior along which control zones and the retail premises are situated. In this way, a grand gateway to Barceloneta is to be obtained and a unique public space created, generated in the land and with the soil to form urban landscapes of differing dimensions.

A text that accompanies E.M.B.T.'s report on the project summarizes in a few sentences and with all the poetry that their projects usually contain the moments and decisions that have played a part in the final result:

"The small scale of Barceloneta... the nearby dwellings and the park... the new high-rise buildings in Barcelona...
It has the verticality of an office tower and the fragmentation of a series of constructions of distinct scales that finally form a unitary volume...
It gives rise to a large projection that forms a grand gateway that can be opened onto Barceloneta...
It forms a unique public space that comes down to the ground and forms an urban landscape of differing dimensions...
The treatment of the facades follows a similar criterion... a series of large windows give it interest from close up... while an undifferentiated volumetric treatment that protects the building from the sun and the noise shows some abstract volumes that become confused with the other constructions along the by-pass."

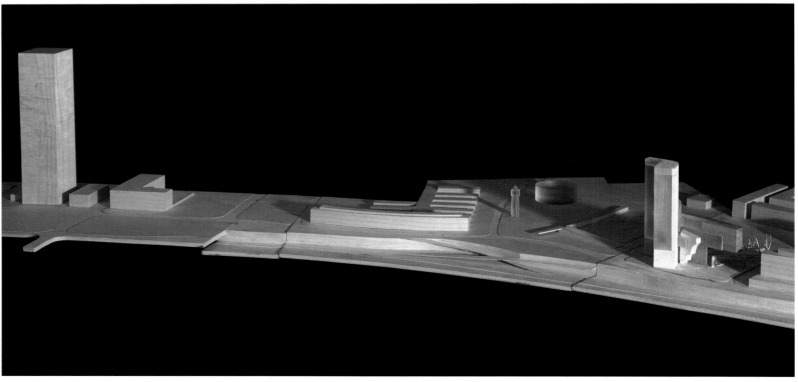

On the previous page, two views of the scale model from different angles are shown. The top one locates the spectator in front of the large corbel and recreates the view that will be enjoyed from the district of Barceloneta.

The bottom one, provides a complete view of the complex as it runs parallel to the Cinturón del Litoral (the city's bypass) in which the idea of a horizontal tower with respect to the vertical tower of the Hotel Arts (on the left-hand side of the photograph) can be appreciated.

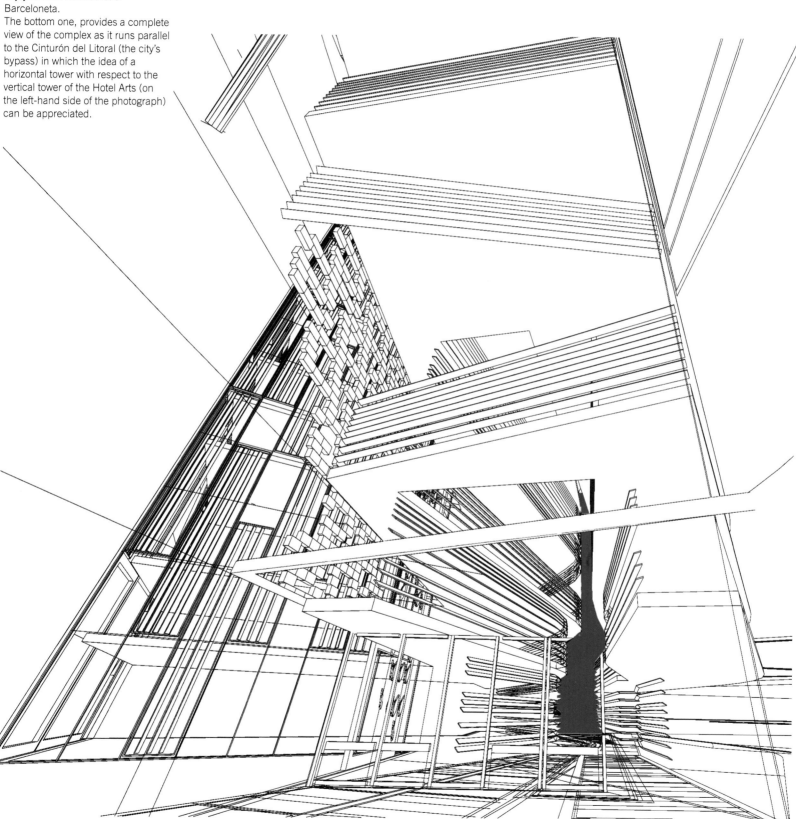

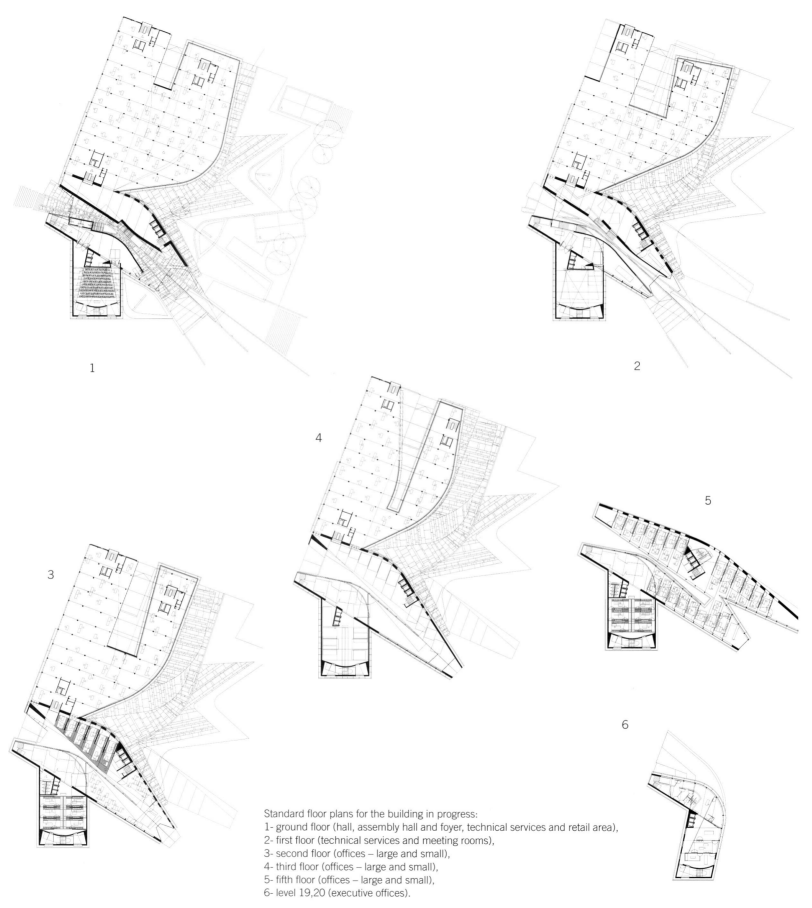

Standard floor plans for the building in progress:
1- ground floor (hall, assembly hall and foyer, technical services and retail area),
2- first floor (technical services and meeting rooms),
3- second floor (offices – large and small),
4- third floor (offices – large and small),
5- fifth floor (offices – large and small),
6- level 19,20 (executive offices).

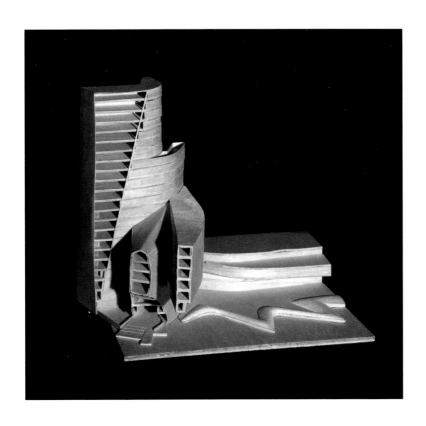

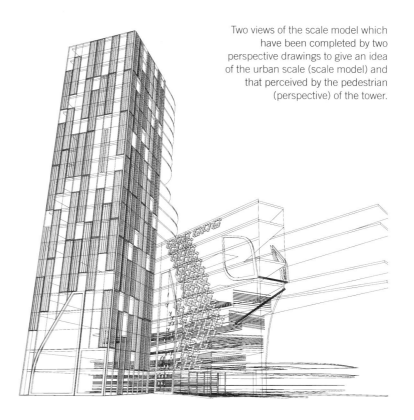

Two views of the scale model which have been completed by two perspective drawings to give an idea of the urban scale (scale model) and that perceived by the pedestrian (perspective) of the tower.

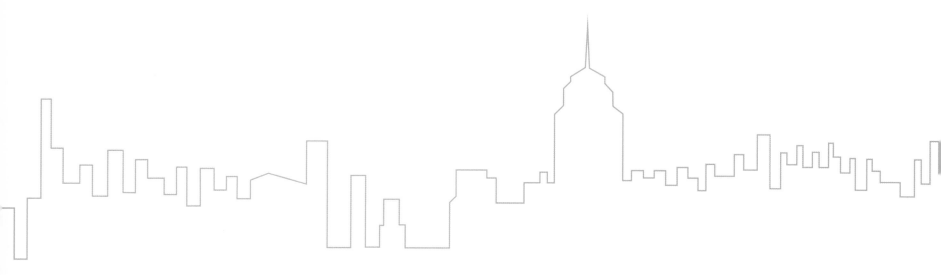

Jean Nouvel was born in 1945 in Fumel (France) and studied architecture in Paris where he graduated in 1972. In 1975, he founded his own studio the Architectures Jean Nouvel (AJN). In 1976, he founded, along with other architects involved in the events of May 68, the Mars 1976 movement. In 1981, he won the competition to construct a series of "great projects" requested by Francois Mitterrand, the French President.

He has been decorated with prestigious rewards such as the Silver Medal by the Académie d'Architecture in 1983, winner of the Grand Prix d'Architecture, Equerre d'Argent in 1987 for the Institut du Monde Arabe (Paris, 1981-87) and in 1993 for the Opera of Lyon (1983-86); the Golden Lion of the Bienale de Venezia in 2000; and the Gold Medal of the Royal Institute of British Architects in 2001. Since 1991 he has been vice-president of the Institut Français d'Arquitecture.

Among his projects under development, we can find the Dentsu Tower in Tokyo, the Hotel Soho in New York, a technological center in Wismar, the social headquarters for Richemont in Geneva, the Quai Branly Museum in Paris, the Philharmonic Concert Hall in Copenhagen, the Guthrie Theater in Minneapolis, the Carnegie Science Center in Pittsburgh and the Guggenheim Museum in Rio de Janeiro.

1987	Institut du Monde Arabe, Paris
1987	Nemausus Public Housing, Nimes
1986	Opera of Lyon, Lyon
1992	Hotel Les Thermes, Dax
1993	Congress Center, Tours
1995	Fondation Cartier, Paris
1995	Galeries Lafayette, Berlin
1999	Auditorium and Conference Center, Lucerna
2000	Town of Justice, Nantes
2003	Torre AGBAR, Barcelona (in collaboration with b720 Arquitectura)

The studio b720 ARQUITECTURA was founded in Barcelona by Fermín Vázquez, Ana Bassat and Adriana Plasencia in 1997. The majority of their work is concentrated in Catalonia, specifically in the city of Barcelona, where they are presently building the AGBAR Tower along side Jean Nouvel and where, briefly, they will be undertaking the design and construction of the "Ciudad justicial" (town of justice) in Barcelona along with David Chipperfield.

Fermín Vázquez has been a visiting lecturer in various universities in Spain and a regular in the design department of the Càtedra Mies van der Rohe of the Escola Tècnica Superior d'Arquitectura de Barcelona. The name of the firm envelops in the abstraction of its acronyms the will to create good unhurried architecture from the city of Barcelona from where the letter b originates. In the universal classification system of matter that constitutes knowledge, we find that the number 7 is the code for the arts and 72 for Architecture within which all its entries are classified as of 720.

1997	Town housing in Tafalla (Navarra)
1997	Complete renovation of residential building in Rambla Catalunya, Barcelona
1998	Office for the Bassat-Ogilvy, Group Barcelona
2000	Residential Building in the Gran Via, Barcelona
2000	Project for the Park of Poblenou, Barcelona (in collaboration with J.Nouvel)
2001	Complete renovation of office building, Barcelona
2003	Torre AGBAR, Barcelona (in collaboration with J.Nouvel)
2003	Project for new access to the Paseo del Ovalo, Teruel (In collaboration with D.Chipperfield)
2004	Project for the extension of the Museum Reina Sofía, Madrid (in collaboration with J.Nouvel)
2007	Project for "Ciudad justicial" (town of justice), Barcelona (in collaboration with D.Chipperfield)

JEAN NOUVEL
Architectures Jean Nouvel

F.VÁZQUEZ, A. BASSAT, A. PLASENCIA
b720 Arquitectura

JEAN NOUVEL +b720 ARQUITECTURA

Architect:

JEAN NOUVEL +b720 ARQUITECTURA

Developer:

Laietana

Structural Engineering:

R. Brufau + A. Obiol

Situation:

Barcelona (Catalonia, Spain)

Project Date:

1999

Completion Date:

2003

Floors:

31

Height:

142 meters

Use:

Offices

This building, in which the central headquarters of the society Aigües de Barcelona (AGBAR [Barcelona's water company]) are to be located, situated obliquely to the Plaça de les Glòries (in the new section of la Avenida Diagonal), will not only be the highest skyscraper to form part of the City of Barcelona's skyline, but it will also be one of the most emblematic due to its elegant, cylindrical-ovoid design. The treatment of the facade, based on a casing of aluminum and crystal, will reflect different tones of color.

The curved form of the floor plan and the irregular channel that surrounds the base of the tower will accentuate the freestanding nature of the tower and involve it in the open space of the plaza. The main pedestrian access to the building is by means of a route that offers a view of the water and vegetation that surround the tower and of the landscaped mineral zone of the plaza with its lunar design. Here, by means of variations in color and in levels, topographical movements are created. The main hall distributes the reception and waiting areas situated on both sides of a vertical nucleus, which is eccentric with curved geometry, that organizes the space and vertical and horizontal circulation. Here, a group of public elevators attached to the radial facade have been situated. A second pedestrian access communicates with the entrance to the auditorium by means of a monumental curved staircase that is located on a lower level. It is illuminated through the waterfalls and artificial lake that fill the channel round the tower's perimeter. In this way, a diffuse light in the interior filtered by water is obtained. This produces reflections on the ceilings of the spaces situated at a lower level such as the three basements situated below the level of the auditorium.

Above the level of access, the building can be divided into two sections: firstly, a concrete shaft of twenty-five standard floors for offices and the like followed by a six-floor glass dome that accommodates the high direc-

TORRE AGBAR

tion and crowns the building. The standard floors have been designed in such a way as to allow for the maximum flexibility in the distribution of the offices, to provide direct views to the exterior and to permit the entrance of natural light. The distribution, apparently fortuitous, of the windows responds to the orientation of the tower and to a fractal composition so that an office orientated to the south or to the west will have fewer openings than one situated in the north or east. The respective thermal benefits are thus regulated and as a result larger apertures are given toward the north and the smallest to the southeast. There is a double facade for the first twenty-five standard floors. This is formed by a structural, interior concrete wall with a finishing based on a colored coating and an exterior skin uniform to the whole building composed of layers of fixed glass with differing inclinations. Between these two skins, which are separated by a distance of 70 cm, maintenance walkways have been installed. The last six floors form the dome with an exterior skin which has a geometric continuity with that of the standard floors.

"It is not a question of a tower, or of a skyscraper in the American sense of the word: it is an emerging volume unique in the middle of a calm city." This is what the architect Jean Nouvel has written to explain the sense of this building inspired in the massif of Montserrat and in the Temple of the Holy Family designed by the local architect Gaudí. Furthermore, a desire to accentuate the singular and symbolic character of a corporate building by the treatment of its covering that fuses the concept of roof and facade in a unique skin is apparent.

Various views of the interior of the tower: the auditorium (top), an office (bottom left) and a waiting area near the elevator bank on the east facade (bottom right). In the interior decoration, the use of a scheme of earthy colors that includes reds stands out. As a result of this, special spaces and atmospheres that are in harmony with the idea of an "architecture that comes from the earth" and that are unexpected in an office building have been created.

Top and bottom. Interior views of the cafeteria and a lobby with waiting area. On the contrary to what actually happens in the interior of the building, an exterior view gives the impression that there is little natural light due to the fact that the outer skin appears to be opaque and the small size of tower's openings.

Top and bottom. Interior view of a floor of offices and the lobby to the auditorium which is reached from the main hall by a circular staircase. *"This is architecture that comes from the Earth, but is not heavy like stone; it could be a distant echo of old formal Catalan obsessions that have their origins in the mysteries of the wind that comes from Montserrat."* (J.Nouvel)

Top and bottom. Interior view of an office and a control room. The spaces that do not need much natural light have been distributed in the north and northeastern zones, and in the south and southwestern zones, the noblest areas with more natural light.

Elevation and west-east section of the tower in which a reading of the tower as being a concrete shaft that rises, in the first 25 floors, parallel to an eccentric rigid nucleus, and a glass cupola, in the last six floors, which do not reach the facade plane, can be made.

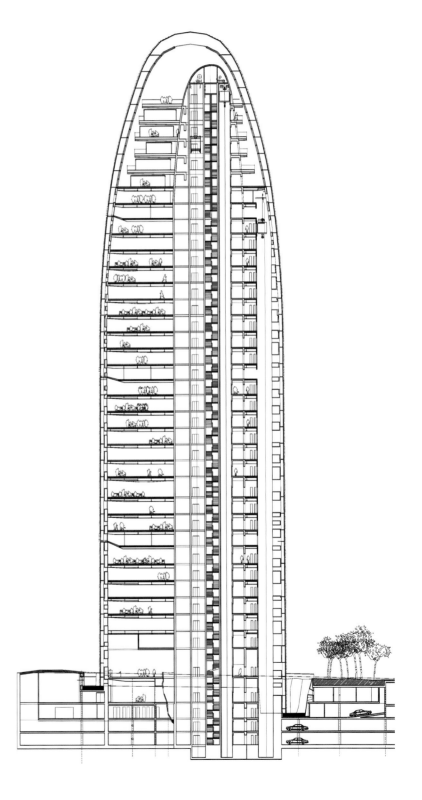

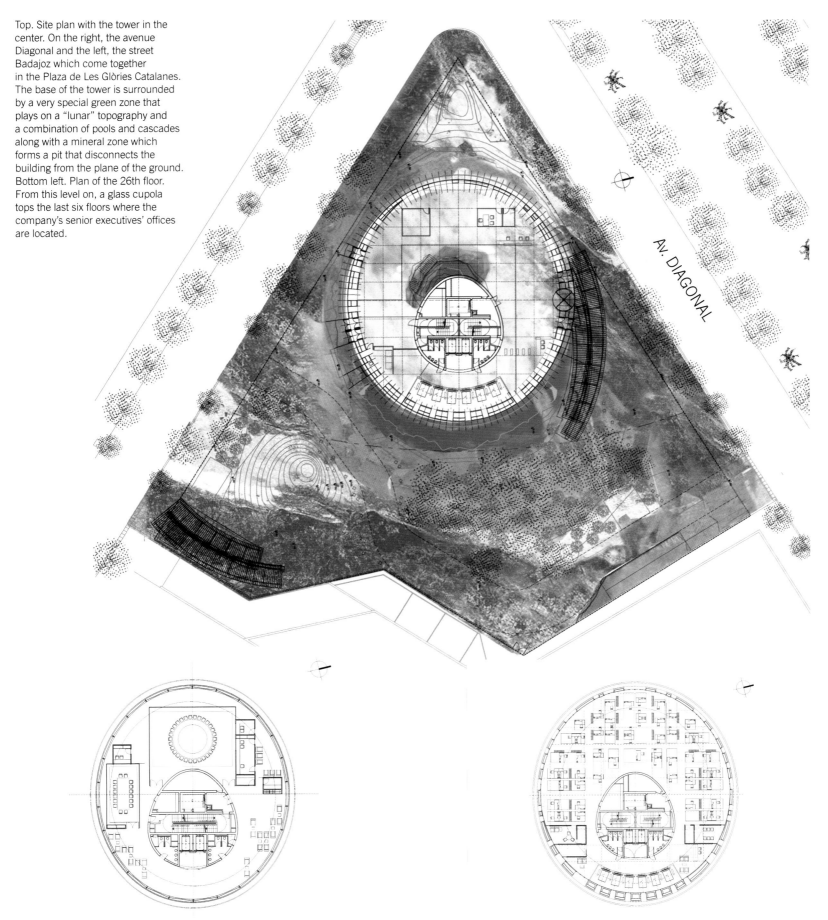

Top. Site plan with the tower in the center. On the right, the avenue Diagonal and the left, the street Badajoz which come together in the Plaza de Les Glòries Catalanes. The base of the tower is surrounded by a very special green zone that plays on a "lunar" topography and a combination of pools and cascades along with a mineral zone which forms a pit that disconnects the building from the plane of the ground. Bottom left. Plan of the 26th floor. From this level on, a glass cupola tops the last six floors where the company's senior executives' offices are located.

AV. DIAGONAL

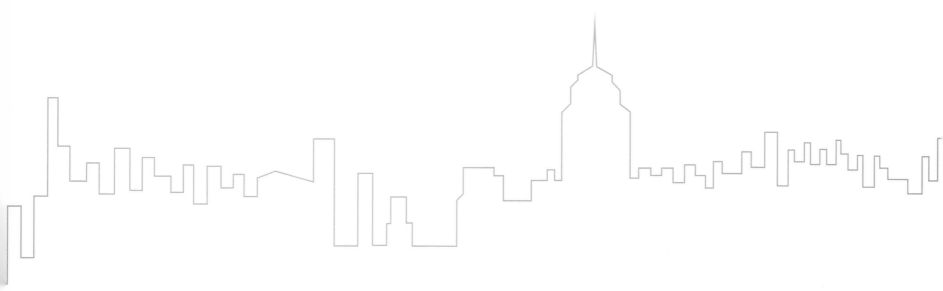

Born in 1926 in Argentina, where he studied architecture, César Pelli moved to the United States in 1956. There, he worked with Eero Saarinen and intervened in projects such as the TWA terminal at JFK Airport (New York). In 1977, he established his own studio: César Pelli & Associates in New Haven (Connecticut). That same year, he was appointed dean of Yale University School of Architecture. This was a post that he held along with that of professor for seven years.

Pelli has become well-known for his rejection of formal preconceptions that condition architecture to a personal style and for this reason, he has constructed buildings for large corporations, public institutions and private clients among which an extensive production of skyscrapers stand out.

In 1999, he published the book Observations for Young Architects in which he explains his conception of architecture. His work has been extensively diffused through monographs, articles and exhibitions. Since 1980, he has been a member of the American Institute of Architects that rewarded him with their gold medal in 1995.

www.cesarpelli.com

1985	World Financial Center Complex, New York
1989	Wells Fargo Center, Minneapolis
1990	181 West Madison, Chicago
1990	777 Tower, Los Angeles
1991	Canary Wharf, London
1991	Carnegie Hall tower, New York
1992	Bank of America Corporate Center, Charlotte (North Carolina)
1995	NTT Head Offices, Shinjuku (Tokyo)
1995	Hotel & Resort Sea Hawk, Fukuoka
1998	Petronas Towers, Kuala Lumpur

CÉSAR PELLI

Cesar Pelli & Associates Architects

Architect:

CESAR PELLI & ASSOCIATES ARCHITECTS

Developers:

Miglin-Beitler Developments

Structural Engineering:

Cohen-Barreto-Marchertas (Chicago)

Situation:

Chicago (Illinois, USA)

Project Date:

1986

Completion Date:

1990

Floors:

50

Height:

184 meters

Use:

Offices

Photography:

Cesar Pelli & Associates

Jon Miller / Hedrich-Blessing

James Yochum

This office tower is found in the Chicago Loop where it stands out due to its square volume that lightly withdraws toward reaching its metallic top. This gesture makes it reconcilable with the city where skyscrapers were born at the end of the 19th century. This also occurs with other buildings by Pelli such as the Bank of America (Charlotte, North Carolina) where the crown at the top reminds us of the sculptural skyscrapers of the beginning of the 20th century such as the Empire State and the Chrysler. César Pelli has developed and brought the architecture of American skyscrapers up to date as a distinguishable architectonic model to be extrapolated from both its positive (efficiency, economy and concentration) and negative aspects (loss of scale and density in the infrastructure).

The majority of the towers that he has designed have been based on a standard floor plan with a central nucleus. This nucleus, which also structural, is basically formed by a set of elevators around which the office space is organized. The remainder of the structure is accentuated with a constant rhythm reflected in the facade by means of vertical ribs faced with granite. A number of stainless steel trimmings suspended beyond the curtain wall of the facade reinforce the scale and the ascending character of the tower. The trunk comes to an end in the final section by the fading away of the facade into narrow stripes that approach the corners in an ascending direction. Each one of these gestures is emphasized with the employment of metal toppings that reflect the light. In addition, at night, with artificial lighting, they make the building stand out in the skyline of the city.

The building can be accessed at ground level through each of the four facades. There is a principle entrance, a secondary and two lateral accesses which transform this space into a great public atrium. The principle entrance is found in Madison Street and it is emphasized by an archway made of glass and metal four floors high that leads the pedestrian into

© Jon Miller / Hedrich-Blessing

181 WEST MADISON

115

Top. Close up of the facade composed of vertical strips of granite, glass and stainless steel.
Bottom from left to right. Photographs of the main entrance and elevator banks in the interior of the large lobby on the ground floor.

the main hall. Designed to be an open and translucent space, basically, glass was used to allow light from outside to enter. To emphasize this sensation of brilliance, light-colored materials such as green, gray and white marbles were employed.

With an extensive professional activity which has led him to work in many different areas, César Pelli considers that a building should be an entity in its own right. He considers that the esthetic qualities should come from the specific characteristics inherent in the initial assignment such as situation, construction techniques applied and function. In the search for the most adequate response for each building, his designs have covered an extensive spectrum of solutions and materials. In this field and, more concretely, in that of technology and the construction industry, this is an aspect that stands out in his works that have been realized. As few contemporary architects have done, he has investigated the economic, technical and expressive possibilities of the coverings of buildings understood as membranes and free of their structural functions.

Top from left to right. Elevation and site plan of the tower that indicates insolation.
Bottom. Ground floor on which entrances to the tower are found in each of the four
facades, the main lobby, the elevator banks and three commercial areas.

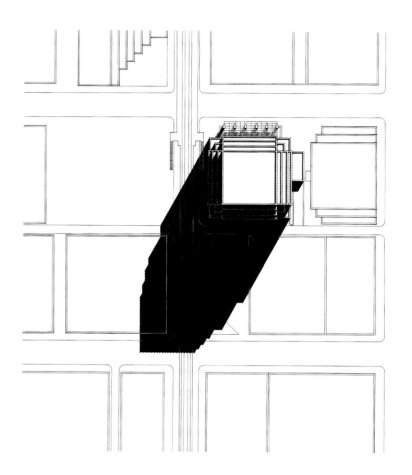

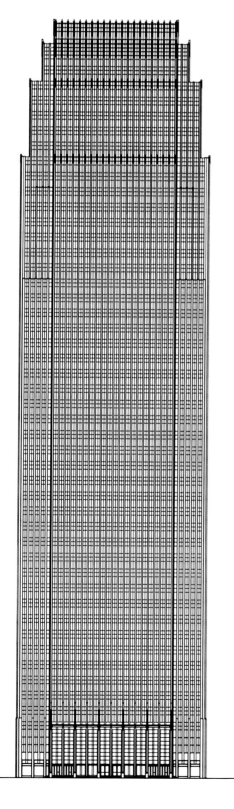

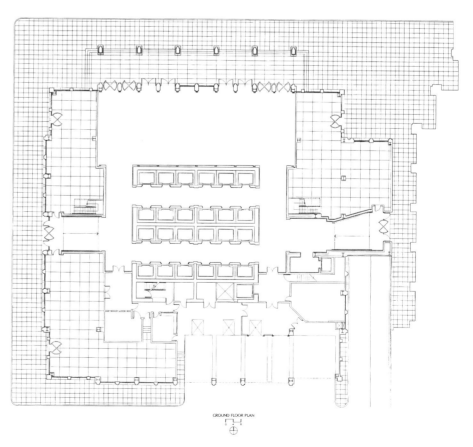

GROUND FLOOR PLAN

Photographs of the glass and steel pergola that is located at a height (approximately four floors) and indicates where the main entrance is situated. It is also an element that offers protection from the weather, transfers the outer public space to a human scale and emphasizes the alignment of the building with respect to the street. This building, which is situated among other high buildings in the Chicago Loop, establishes mechanisms that provide references at a pedestrian level.

© Jon Miller / Hedrich-Blessing

© Jon Miller / Hedrich-Blessing

Architect:

CESAR PELLI & ASSOCIATES ARCHITECTS

Developers:

NationsBank Corporation,
Charter Properties & Lincoln Property Co.

Structural Engineering:

W. P. Moore & Ass.

Situation:

Charlotte (North Carolina, USA)

Project Date:

1987

Completion Date:

1992

Floors:

60

Height:

265.5 meters

Use:

Offices

Photography:

Timothy Hursley
Cesar Pelli & Associates

This building that is also known as the NationsBank Corporate Center (given that this is the name of the entity that promoted its construction) in addition to being the corporate headquarters of the Bank of America, concentrates a great diversity of services in its base. It is found in the economic, historic and geographical center of the city of Charlotte where it is a point of reference and the highest building (to date) in the southeast of the United States.

Its construction responded as much to the economic viability for the developer (maximum height, functional efficacy and cost saving) as to the possibility of revitalizing the urban center of the city culturally and economically. César Pelli understood how to undertake this assignment and came up with a proposal of a functional and architectonic nature that went far beyond the economic factors and generated a great public complex of which the tower of the Bank of America is the corner stone.

A series of public uses have been integrated into the program for the building. The ground floor occupies the complete block and creates the complex that comprises a hotel, two theaters, two landscaped gardens and the Founders Hall - a civic and commercial center - in the heart of the tower. Designed as a large atrium covered by a rectangular skylight that organizes the public space around its perimeter and distributes the retail areas, the two halls for the North Carolina Performing Arts Center and the pedestrian entrances to the tower. In an annex on the block behind the complex, there is a public car park connected to the interior of the Founders Hall by means of a walkway that crosses the street. In the same way, two more walkways connect the blocks on each side with the interior of the complex.

The tower also possesses a direct access from the outside that can be reached through a small landscaped garden that highlights the importance

© T. Hursley

of the construction and avoids the necessity for a large independent frontal access. The classical use of volume and the elegance of the tower is enhanced by its crowning that consists of an assembly of aluminum bars that reflects the light of the sun during the day and emits sparkles when it is subject to nocturnal lighting. The curved lines of the floor plan stand out and define a volume that reminds us of the classical American skyscrapers of the 20's and 30's.

The base, wrapped in dark granite, creates an image of solidity and the trunk ascends vertically in horizontal bands of beige granite interrupted by the holes of the windows that form a square-grid that goes on progressively narrowing following the stepping in of the facade. In contrast to the monolithic character of this section, the upper floors become lighter. The main facades curve slightly and are projected toward the interior as the tower gains in height to culminate with a crown that has earned the nickname of "the queen of the city" from the citizens of Charlotte.

Regarding the image of the building and its architectural conception, César Pelli has manifested: *"Charlotte is a city that is being redefined. It is almost new. Only a few old buildings exist. So it was a question of writing on a blackboard that was almost clean. The objective was not so much that of referring to a specific context as to building a beautiful tower that would transmit a fitting impression of the NationsBank Corporate Center".*

Top. Close up of one of the ground-floor entrances from an exterior public area with water fountains.
Bottom from left to right. Two shots of the tower: nocturnal view in which the tower stands out from the other building in the city due to the illumination of its top floors; detail of the top of the tower.

Views of the interior of the tower.
Top. Detail of an interior passageway between the elevator banks in which the zenithal illumination has been created by the installation of leaded lights.
Bottom. A lobby on a standard floor which gives access to the elevator banks and offices.

© T. Hursley

© T. Hursley

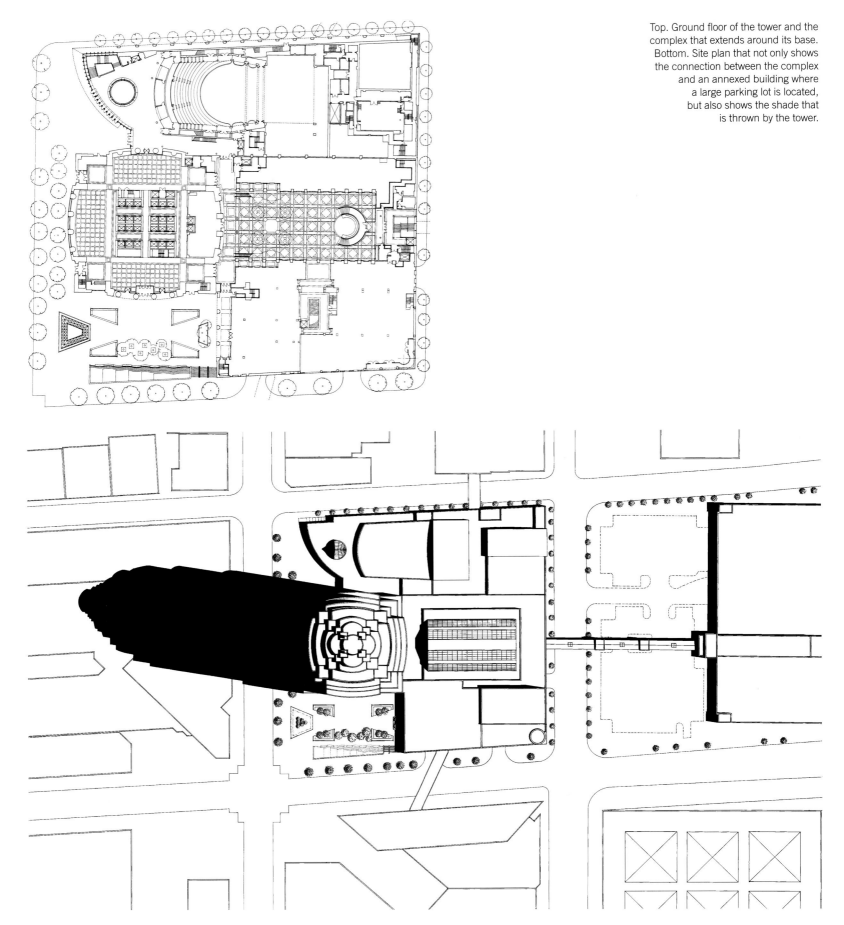

Top. Ground floor of the tower and the complex that extends around its base. Bottom. Site plan that not only shows the connection between the complex and an annexed building where a large parking lot is located, but also shows the shade that is thrown by the tower.

From left to right. Elevation. Nocturnal view of the tower in which the topping stands out. Thanks to this element that has been manufactured from circular pieces of stainless steel, the tower stands out as much as by day as by night.
Inferior. The tower as seen in its surroundings. It is a modern building that pays tribute to the American architecture of the 19th Century.

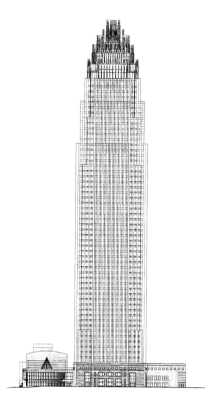

© Cesar Pelli & Associates

© T. Hursley

125

CÉSAR PELLI

CÉSAR PELLI

Architect:

CESAR PELLI & ASSOCIATES ARCHITECTS

Developers:

Kuala Lumpur City Center Sendirian Berhad (KLCCB)

Structural Engineering:

Thornton-Tomaseti

+ Ranhill Bersekutu

Situation:

Kuala Lumpur, Malaya

Project Date:

1992

Completion Date:

1998

Floors:

88

Height:

452 meters

Use:

Offices and services

Photography:

Jeff Goldberg / Esto

Malaysia is the Asian country in the Basin (a zone in the Pacific) that has undergone the fastest process of industrial development and growth. Evidence of this hegemony is found in the capital where the highest building in the world has been built. For the first time in the race for the heights, a building has been raised outside of the United States. As skyscrapers are still symbols of economic power, we find that the main occupant of the Petronas Towers is the national petroleum company (called Petronas) that belongs to the federal government.

Situated in a central commercial district of Kuala Lumpur, they form part of a project for general urban planning promoted by the government to provide floor space in the city. The Kuala Lumpur City Center (KLCC), objective of an international competition won by the architect César Pelli, occupies a 5.7-hectare site within the lands occupied by the established Selangor Turf Club. The proposal was based on the idea of building "a city within a city" where residential use is combined with offices, commercial areas, hotels and spaces for cultural activities. With the expectation of attracting near to 50,000 people a day to the center, the necessary infrastructures were created: a train station for light transportation; underpasses; widening of highway accesses and an underground parking lot for 4,500 vehicles. Approximately, half of the land is destined to public space so that parks and gardens surround the central axis of the proposal. The two symmetrical eighty-eight-floor towers have an outer casing of stainless steel. They are connected (and decorated) by a bridge anchored by means of inclined supports which form, as described symbolically by César Pelli, a "gateway to the heavens".

In response to the conditions laid down for the competition that encouraged a form of architecture that would reflect and relate to the physical and cultural aspects of the country, such as the tropical climate and Islamic culture, the project for the towers was developed with the Malaysian

TORRES PETRONAS

Top. Axonometric drawing of the two-story bridge that connects the two towers and includes its inclined structural support.
Bottom from left to right. Detail of the footbridge as seen from the street and a frontal shot taken from a height. The entire building is clad in stainless steel.

identity in mind. The floor plan is developed from the turn and superimposition of two squares that are connected by means of small circular fillings (motifs inspired in traditional Islamic decoration that also respond to modern concepts). This is reproduced in the exterior in the form of a cylinder that rises parallel to the towers to the 42nd floor. Here the towers are connected by means of a high vestibule and bridge. The towers are set in the framework of a concrete perimeter tube, 46 m in diameter, and connected by filled diaphragms that absorb the vertical loads. The horizontal loads are transmitted to the center of the columns that are fixed to the perimeter tube at the corners.

The exterior treatment (the design of the volumes and facade) is innovative, functional and one of the buildings most characteristic aspects. The shadows cast on the ground by the towers project a silhouette that recalls popular architecture and the reflections from the stainless steel represent the wealth and richness of Malaysian culture. The Petronas Towers express as much the traditional local culture as the dynamism of the emerging Malaysian economy as their roots have been set in ancestral grounds and they denote the challenges that the future presents.

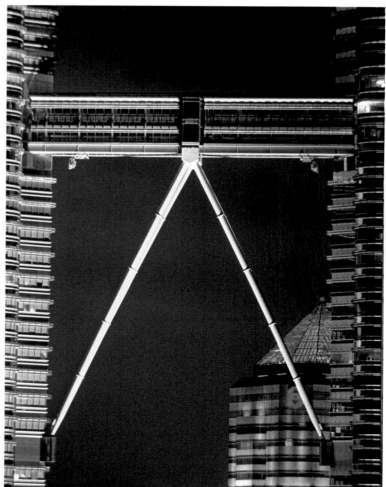

Top. Detail of the towers and bridge at the height of the 42nd floor.
Bottom left. The towers in their urban surroundings.
Bottom right. Detail of the pinnacle of one of the towers. The cylindrical volumes that accompany the shaft from the ground floor stop at the 42nd floor where they coincide with the level of the bridge. A lobby is situated at this height.
Following page. Photograph of the ground floor level taken from the boulevard from where there are pedestrian entrances to the towers and to the large complex known as Kuala Lumpur City Center (KLCC) that has been developed in the base.

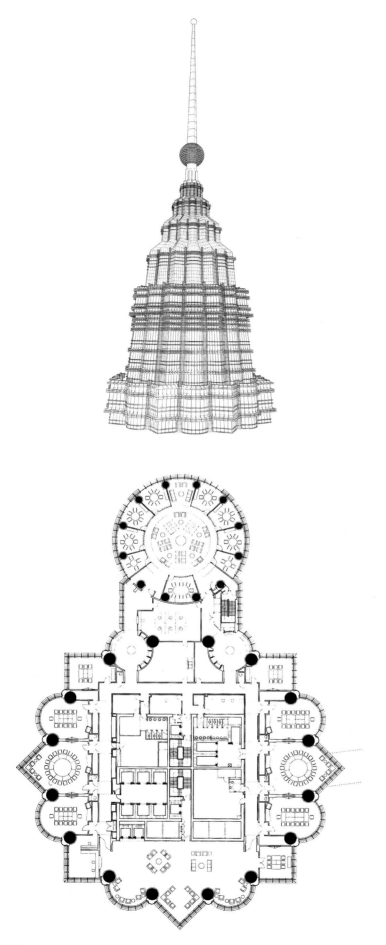

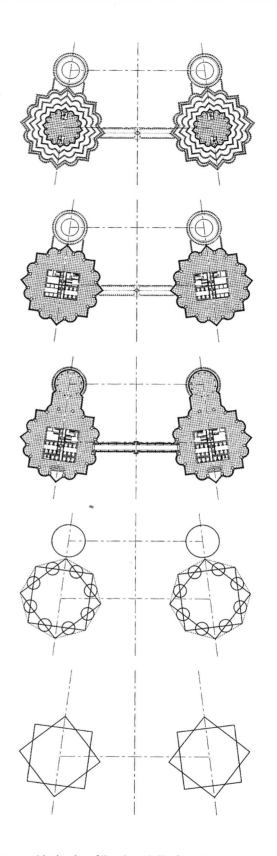

Top left. Axonometric drawing of the pinnacle like form that crowns the towers.
Bottom left. Standard floor plan up to level 42 where the cylindrical form finishes.
The spatial distribution has been organized around a central nucleus
and the structural elements distributed around the perimeter of the facade.
Above. Geometric development of the floor plan that has been based on
the superimposition and rotation of one square by 45° over another; the inclusion
of a cylindrical form; the standard floor plan for the first 42 stories; those that follow
and go on to the top; and one of the last levels.

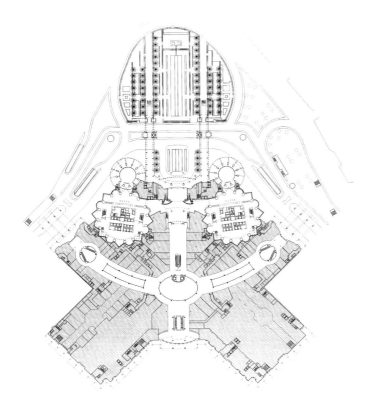

Site plan of the ground floor level of the Kuala Lumpur City Center complex. The towers form a gateway that gives access, from a large boulevard, to the large 140,000 m² complex dedicated to retail centers and entertainment and that has been developed along the lines of a great podium.

CÉSAR PELLI

Architect:

CESAR PELLI &
ASSOCIATES ARCHITECTS

Developers:

Bizkaiko Foru Aldundia

Situation:

Bilbao (The Basque Country, Spain)

Project Date:

2002

Floors:

31

Height:

160 meters

Use:

Offices

In 1993, the City Council of Bilbao held an international competition for the presentation of ideas for the urban development of the Abandoibarra area. The architect César Pelli won with a General Plan which provides a balance between private and public interests and relates well to the existing city. In addition to being the capital of Vizcaya, it is also the cultural, social and business center of the Basque Country. Due to its privileged situation, Abandoibarra will make it possible for the present center of Bilbao to extend toward the river Nervión that will cease to be a barrier to the expansion of the city. To recuperate this space that is found between the river and the suburban development, the existing urban axes have been prolonged along with the incorporation of new streets that favor open public spaces and pedestrian needs with regard to the use of the private vehicle.

Totally regenerating the one-kilometer space that extends along the riverside between two of the main cultural foci of the city (the Guggenheim Museum and the Palacio Euskalduna de Congresos y de la Música) a new metropolitan center on the banks of the river Nervión will be created. This will constitute a seafront environment consisting of more than 200,000 m2 of green zones and new plots available for the development of offices, the commercial center Zubiarte by the North American architect Robert Stern, the Sheraton Hotel by the Mexican Ricardo Legorreta, university installations and living spaces (of which the first building of the Basque architect Luís Peña Ganchegui is currently under construction).

The Torre Diputación 2002 where the new headquarters of the Bizkaiko Foru Aldundia (the local governmental authorities of Bizkaia) will be located will be the main element of the General Plan for Abandoibarra due to its central position and height. It will be Bilbao's highest building and an important landmark as it will be distinguishable from any point of the city. It will be situated in the new Plaza Euskadi where it meets the exist-

DIPUTACIÓN 2002

ing suburban development as a result of the prolongation of the calle Elkano. The building's vocation for public use is manifested by its functional organization. There is to be a base four floors in height that will extend all the way around the plaza. In the interior of this podium, suspended ramps are to be located parallel to the facade which will reinforce the oval form of the plaza and permit the public to circulate vertically in the interior of the building as if it were an extension of the city.

The floor plan of the tower is triangular although its sides are slightly curved. The volume is to be gracefully elevated and will incline progressively as it gains height and evokes a glass obelisk. For the initial project, César Pelli designed a tower with 40 floors which he has had to reduce to 31. However, the architect has not wanted to give up on the initial tower and these floors have been gained virtually with a careful use of perspective. He has constructed a tower that is, in potential, a great deal higher than it really is and in which if we were to prolong the lines of the arrises, we would be able to imagine how they converged in a point in infinity to form an obelisk. In this way, the architect has conceived a building that will reach the heavens when viewed favorably and this has added sensitivity to his architecture.

Top. Perspective from calle Elkano.
The axis that extends from the
present city towards the tower
is the main reference point
for Abandoibarra's new urban
development.
Bottom. Detail from the interior
of the podium of the tower. This is
a large public area that is developed
around the oval movement
of the plaza.

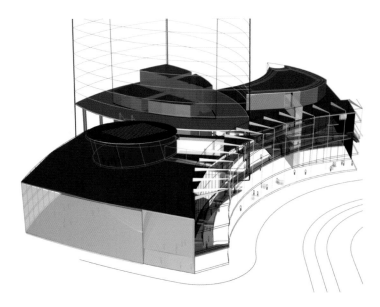

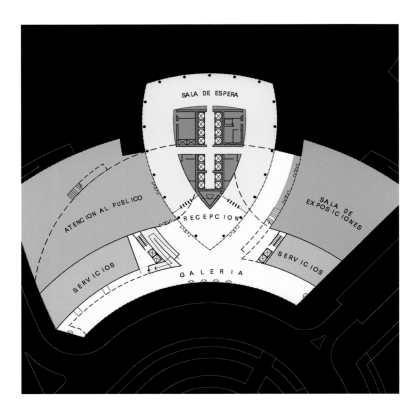

Top left. Axonometric impression of the base of the tower and its starting point.
Top right. Ground and access floor to the tower and podium that has been developed over two levels. The uses of the areas have been indicated in different colors. The standard floor structure of the tower that is distributed around a central nucleus is also shown. Center. Longitudinal section of the base in which the main functions have been indicated by the use of different colors.
Bottom. Longitudinal section of the base and the tower.

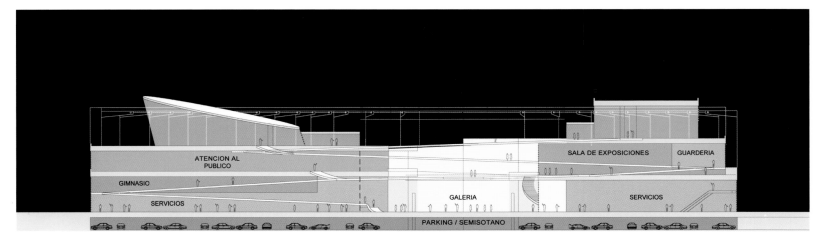

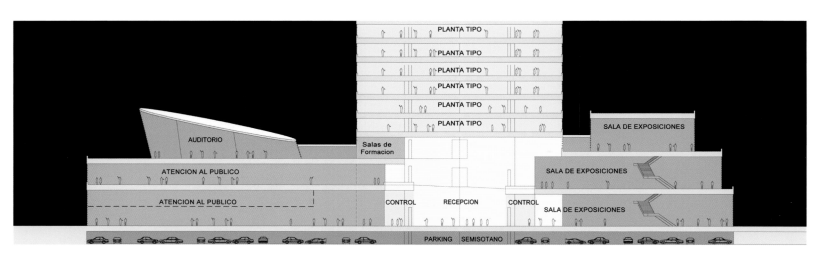

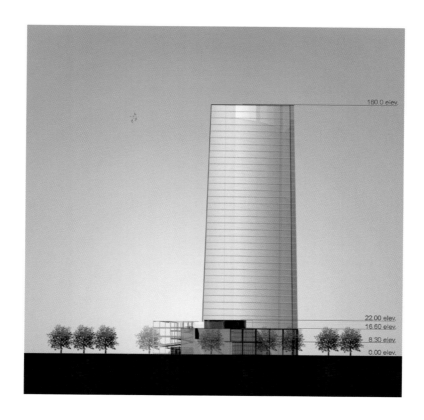

Top and bottom. Elevations of the right side and front of the tower. The facade is a glass skin that covers the entire building that has been defined by its composition based on horizontal strips.

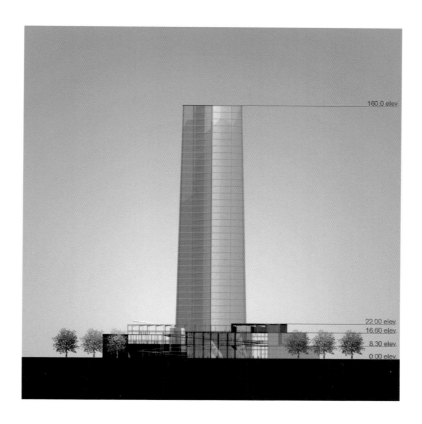

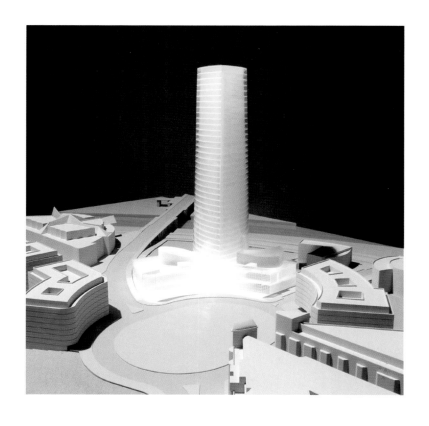

Top and bottom. View of the scale model of the projected urban planning scheme for the area of Abandoibarra in the proximity of the River Nervión. The project has been based around a central point of reference, the Plaza Euskadi, where the new Bizkaiko Foru Aldundia (Foral Delegation of Bizkaia) tower will be situated along with the prolongation of an existing urban axis, the calle Elkano.

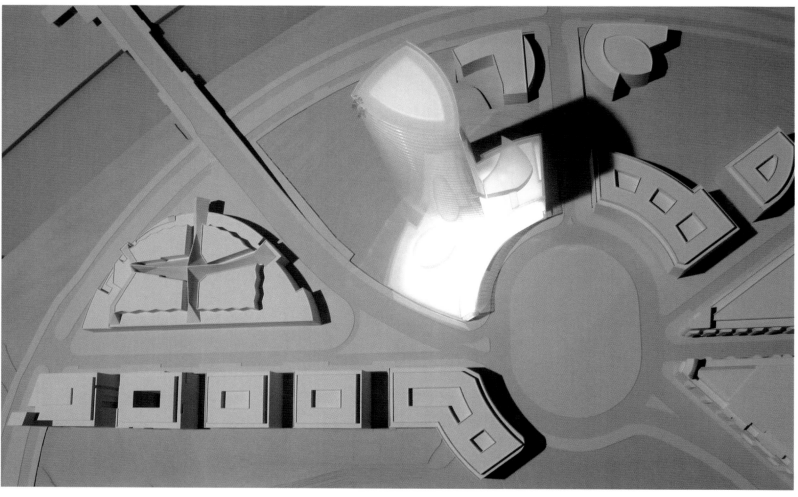

Top. The tower as seen from the plaza. Due to its central position and height (once constructed, it will be the highest building in Bilbao), it will be the principal element in this new zone that is to become the motor of the city.
Bottom. Close up of the podium of the tower where the main public functions will be accommodated. The curvilinear glass facade and the ramps, that completely surround the building, emphasize the sensation of dynamism that the rhythm of the city stamps on the lives of its citizens.

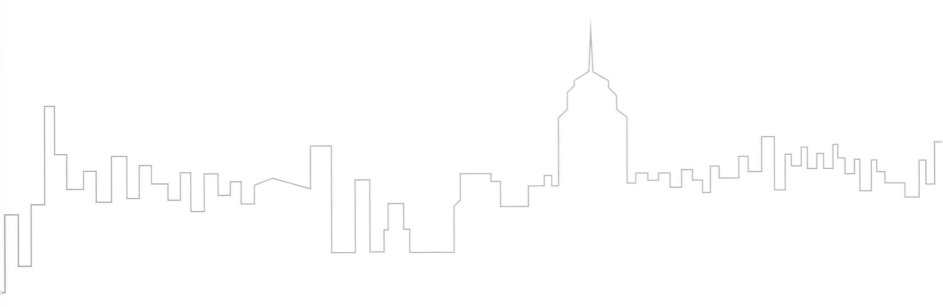

Renzo Piano was born in Rome in 1937. He graduated in 1964 at the Polytechnic of Milan and completed his formation with visits to England and the United States between 1965 and 1970. It was during these trips that he came to meet Jean Prouvé whose friendship has been a great influence on his professional life.

In 1971, he founded the studio Piano & Rogers along with Richard Rogers with whom he built the Centre Georges Pompidou in Paris in 1977. Later, he created the studio Atelier Piano & Rice with the engineer Peter Rice. This collaboration lasted until Rice's death in 1993. It was then that he founded the present Renzo Piano Building Workshop which has offices in Paris and Genoa and where more than 100 people work. The staff is formed by architects (some of who are associates), engineers, and other specialists.

As outstanding recent works we can list: the NEMO Museum of Science and Technology (Amsterdam), the Debis Building and various other buildings in the Daimler Benz Postdamer Platz (Berlin), the Centre Cultural Jean Marie Tjibaou (New Caledonia) and the office and apartment building Aurora Place (Sydney).

www.rpwf.org

1977	Centre Pompidou, París (in collaboration with Richard Rogers)
1983	Olivetti Building, Napoles
1994	Kansai International Airport, Osaka (in collaboration with Nikken Sekkei Ltd)
1997	Reconstruction of Brancusi's Workshop, París
1997	Museum of Science and technology NEMO, Amsterdam
1997	The Debis Building (Central Offices Daimler Benz) Berlin
1998	Cultural Center Jean Marie Tjibaou, Nouméa
1998	Daimler Benz Potsdamer Platz. Music Hall, Imax, Residencies and retail center, Berlin
2000	KPN Tower Telecom, Rotterdam
2000	Office and residential Building Aurora Place, Sydney

RENZO PIANO
Renzo Piano Building Workshop

RENZO
PIA

Architect:

RENZO PIANO
BUILDING WORKSHOP

Developers:

Ove Arup & Partners

Structural Engineering:

Lend Lease Design Group

Situation:

Sydney (Australia)

Project Date:

1996

Completion Date:

2000

Floors:

44

Height:

200 meters

Use:

Offices and Residencies

Photography:

John Gollings / RPBW

Lend Lease / Martin Van Der Wal

This complex of buildings was to be finalized in the year 2000 to coincide with the celebration of the Sydney Olympic Games. The developers' desire was to construct an emblematic building for mixed usage. Although it was a private development, the architect Renzo Piano invited the local authorities and public opinion to become involved in the project. The tower would be a homage to the city. It was to be more of a landmark than simply another skyscraper.

The final design consists of two buildings, a 44-floor office tower that is connected to a 17-floor residential block. The result is an architectural group that relates to the city and recounts its urban transformation from the uniform scale of the residential weave to the modern office towers of the financial district close to the historic center. Related to the public space by means of a covered plaza (by a canvas suspended by steel cables) that has been created between them, they induce an urban microcosm.

It is situated in a historic neighborhood of the city (in which a new network of skyscrapers is being imposed) in front of the Royal Botanical Gardens, a large park that is in front of the Opera House. Designed by the architect Jorn Utzon and built between 1957 and 1973 on an extremity of the bay, it is one of the symbols of the city due to its characteristic form and the gateway function it fulfils. Aurora Place seeks to yield homage to this building placing special attention on its architecture and transmitting two elements of Australian culture that are also found in Utzon's building: the wind and the sea. The elliptical form of the ground plan reminds us of a ship's hull and the glass skin that forms the outer casing reinforces this image. Elevated, the planes of the facade look like gigantic sails that wave in the wind as do the coverings of the Opera House.

The design of the tower is based on the layout of: a central nucleus of reinforced concrete where the elevator banks, emergency stairs, services and

© John Gollings / RPBW

installations are situated. This element is the backbone of the building which is complemented with a plane of circular pillars set parallel to the facade and that follow the curved form of the floor plan. The standard floor plan is open in as much that it is adaptable to the necessities of different users given that the tower is directed towards rented offices. The residential building follows the same scheme of a central nucleus, accumulating structure and services which leaves the entire perimeter of the main facades free. In addition, each one of the apartments has a terrace with views of the port and the park.

The main facades cover the building by means of a curtainwall (interrupted on the sides) that on reaching the roof does not stop immediately, but continues to take in installations and other volumes. The lateral facades, two bands of terracotta, are set back and form a second skin that covers the walls of the tower.

The exterior image manifests the original idea that proposed a building as a singular element in dialogue with its surroundings from its form to the composition of the facade.

From an urbanistic and sociocultural point of view, the Aurora Place Complex is an example of how it can be positive to relate two uses that have traditionally tended to be separated such as those of offices and living spaces. Winter gardens and terraces with exceptional views of the port function as spaces for leisure available to all the users of the complex who seek an interrelationship between work zones and residential areas. It has been by provoking this constant activity that the building has been prevented from becoming a mere container that fills and empties according to the rhythm of a working timetable that would create an empty sensation for the residents. The links that have been created among the historic neighborhood, the park and the bay emphasize the playful character that this building with a social vocation has.

Top left. Aurora Place as seen from the bay and forming part of the city facade behind the Royal Botanical Gardens.
Bottom left. View of both of the buildings that form the complex from Macquarie Street in the historical center of the city. The residential 17-story building transmits an urban scale while the office tower relates more to the profile of the emerging financial district.
Bottom right. Detail of the curtainwall that extends beyond the constructed volume. This tops the tower and hides, at the same time, installations and technical elements that have been situated on the roof.

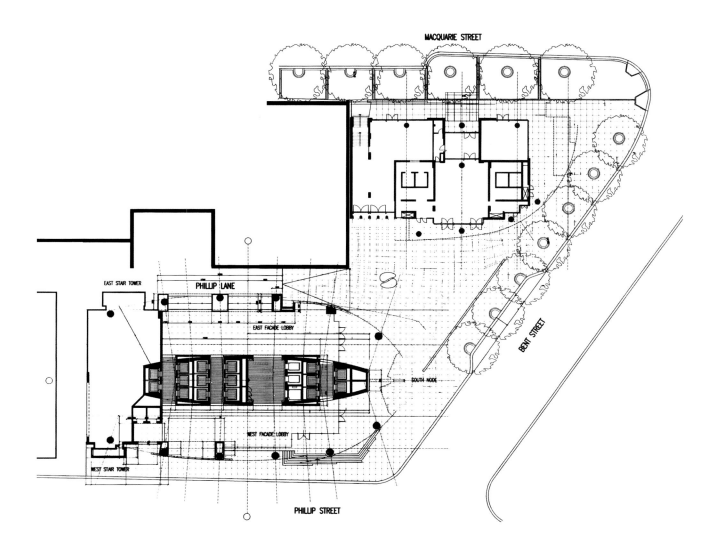

MACQUARIE STREET

EAST STAIR TOWER

PHILLIP LANE

EAST FACADE LOBBY

BENT STREET

SOUTH NODE

WEST FACADE LOBBY

WEST STAIR TOWER

PHILLIP STREET

Ground floor of the complex.
On this level, common public spaces
such as pedestrian entrances, retail
areas and the plaza, which has been
created between the two buildings and
is partially covered by means
of a canvas anchored by
steel cables, can be accessed
from Macquarie Street.
Bottom. Standard floor plan
for the office tower that is characterized
by its formal clarity: the central structural
nucleus defines the distribution of the
interior and characterizes the volume
of the building.

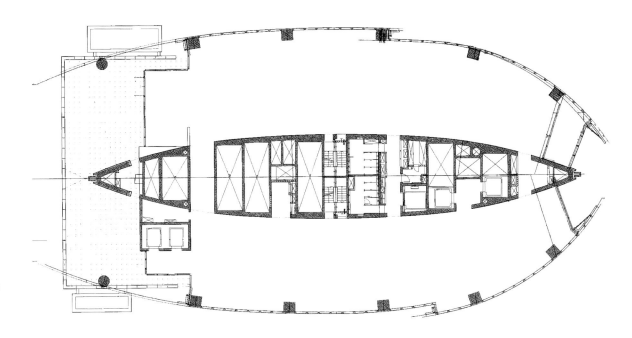

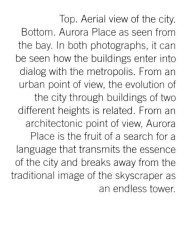

Top. Aerial view of the city. Bottom. Aurora Place as seen from the bay. In both photographs, it can be seen how the buildings enter into dialog with the metropolis. From an urban point of view, the evolution of the city through buildings of two different heights is related. From an architectonic point of view, Aurora Place is the fruit of a search for a language that transmits the essence of the city and breaks away from the traditional image of the skyscraper as an endless tower.

Top. View of the Bay of Sydney from the heights of the building. In the foreground, the covering that extends beyond the height of the facade. Bottom. View of the Bay of Sydney with the Opera House by the architect Jørn Utzon in the foreground. Behind, numerous high buildings that comprise the financial district can be seen. Among them is Aurora Place in which the elliptical form of the floor plan and the curtainwall of the facade seek complicity with J.Utzon's building, the symbol of the city.

© John Gollings / RPBW

© John Gollings / RPBW

Detail of one of the ground-floor entrances in the residential building. The facade is composed of a curtainwall that is technical (it regulates a series of functions) and formal. It confers a misty image to the building in its higher areas and plays on the reflections and contrasts from the Macquarie Street facade. Bottom from left to right. Photograph of the east facade, elevations south, north and west.

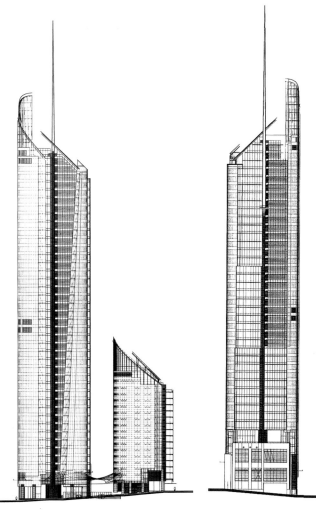

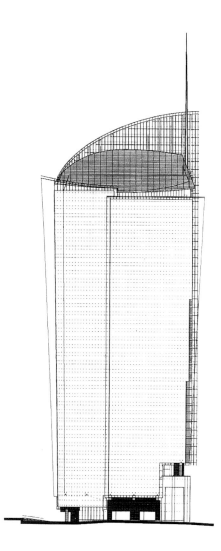

Top. Photograph taken from the interior of the residential tower. The curtainwall is a technical element that regulates itself according to the incidence of solar rays and the temperature of the walls of the building. Bottom. Photograph of the north side of the building taken from street level.

Born in Casablanca (Morocco) in 1944, Christian de Portzamparc graduated in 1969 as an architect in Paris in the Ecole des Beaux-Arts. The majority of his projects that have reached the stage of construction are found in France such as the water tower in Marne-la-Vallee. Here, he was able to articulate his concept of a new urban landscape based on the biblical Tower of Babel. His international activity started after he won the 1984 competition for the City of Music in Vilette Park, Paris (this was completed in 1995 and consists of a group of structures situated around the border of Vilette Park) and was consolidated by his participation in the construction of an apartment building in Fukuoka (Japan, 1982-92).

He has been awarded the medal of the Académie Française d'Architecture (1992) and the Grand Prix National de l'Architecture (1993). In 1994, he received one of the most important international awards, the Pritzker Prize, as universal recognition for his professional development and for the way in which he has responded to the specifics of the urban surroundings in each of his projects.

He is currently constructing the new French Embassy in Berlin, a concert hall in Luxembourg, a cultural area in Rennes and an apartment building in Grenoble.

www.chdeportzamparc.com

1979	Water Castle, Marne-la-Vallée
1992	Apartment Building Nexus World, Fukuoka
1995	City of Music, Paris
1995	Crédit Lyonnais Tower, Euralille (Lille)
1999	LVMH Office Tower, New York
2000	The Law Courts Building, Grasse, la Provenza
2000	Grande Bibliotheque du Quebec, Montreal
2002	French Embassy Building, Berlín
2003	Cultural Area in Rennes, Brittany
2000	New Philharmonic Hall, Luxembourg

CHRISTIAN DE PORTZAMPARC
Atelier Christian de Portzamparc

CHRISTIA
DE PORTZ

Architect:

CHRISTIAN DE PORTZAMPARC

Developers:

LVMH

Structural Engineering:

Weiskops and Pickworth

Situation:

New York (New York, USA)

Project Date:

1995

Completion Date:

1999

Floors:

24

Height:

100 meters

Use:

Offices

Photography:

Nicolas Borel

The LVMH tower is the corporate headquarters of the French firm of luxury articles Louis Vuitton and Moët Hennessy. As promoters, they expressed a desire to raise a building that would represent the new forms and expressions of contemporary architecture as a reflection of the enterprise's commercial profile in the American market. It is situated on a narrow plot with very little facade on 57th Street near its crossing with Madison Avenue in Manhattan. It is placed in a breach between two buildings from different periods and of different styles, between the gray granite of Chanel and the redbrick of the Chemical Bank. In addition to the surroundings, another point to be taken into account when starting the project was the urbanistic regulation for the area of the city known as "sun and shadow". This ordinance has characterized a large number of the classic and emblematic skyscrapers of New York as it leads buildings to step inwards as they gain in height. Finally, a relatively low, narrow, adjacent building was to be respected. This property was later acquired by the promoter and a slight increase in surface obtained.

In the first sketches for the project, a play of cubic and cylindrical volumes in a very narrow facade was experimented with. In the evolution toward the final proposal, Christian de Portzamparc defined the building as a tower with a flat facade that was transformed into volume when treated as a skin. This has been doubled into planes like a gigantic lily so that the front of the facade opens up as if it were petals protecting the heart of a flower. The floors also reflect this movement of the exterior closing as it draws a perimeter that oscillates and folds on itself. The search toward a design for a discontinuous facade that offered formal personality to the building also solved the problem of the possibility of the building being nullified by its urban surroundings. A classical flat glass facade would lead to the building becoming a mirror reflecting the buildings situated in front of it such as the green granite building of IBM.

The curtainwall of this building is unconventional. Its design stems from a horizontal rectangular weft that combines trapezoidal panels with two different

TORRE LVMH

© Nicolas Borel

treatments on the glass: when the glass plane reaches its encounters with the false ceiling it has a reduced iron content and is screen printed with white horizontal bands which are combined with others of an inverse proportion created by sandblasting to obtain a translucent effect. This treatment not only contributes to evading the mirror effect, but also to creating quality surroundings in the work places from which the city is perceived through a sieve with different degrees of transparency. At the same time, the interior lighting and the nocturnal treatment that is given to the building uses pastel green and violet tones which emphasize the idea of the building being a great lily even more, a flower in the middle of the great metropolis, in the middle of the agitated life of Manhattan.

The LVMH is a tower among "shared walls" in the dense fabric of the center of the city. Christian de Portzamparc's task was to resolve how to raise an icon in that difficult location conditioned by diverse circumstances. The final solution has been found in a poetic gesture that inverts the initial factors (such as the forced staggered vertical growth) and obtains the gesture that makes it so identifiable.

The building as seen by pedestrians from East 57th Street. The tower is not a building of great proportions given that it is located on a very narrow plot and surrounded by other buildings. As a consequence, the tower plays with a delicate glass skin that falls back as it gains height.

From left to right. Standard floor plans
of the tower which are characterized
by the way in which the functional
elements do not interrupt the
continuity of the space and allow
for, in this way, numerous possible
distributions to suit the necessities
of the users of the offices.
In this series of levels, the way in
which the volume of the building
changes can be observed. This
movement is accompanied by
the fold in the facade.

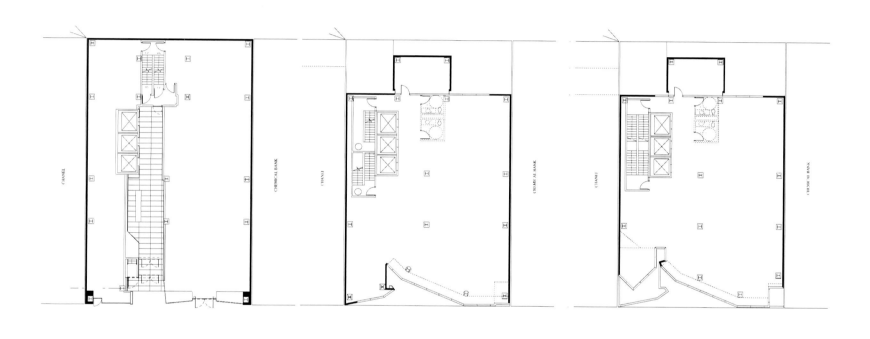

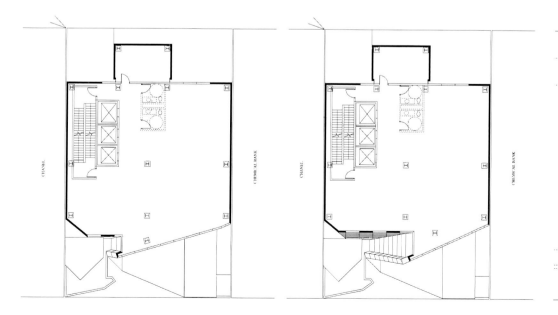

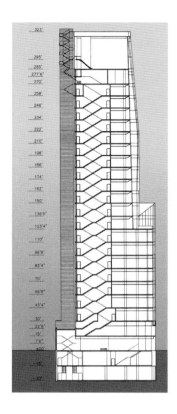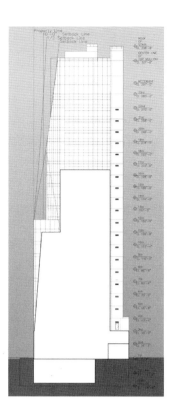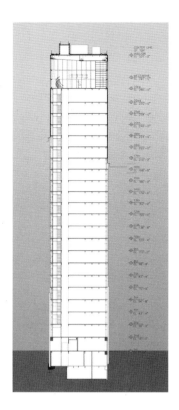

Top from left to right. Sections and elevations.
Bottom left. Sketch of one of the moments of the project by Christian de Portzamparc. The use of watercolor emphasizes the idea of the building as a poetic, delicate image.
Bottom right. Site plan of the tower that shows how it is located on a heterogeneous block. Sun and shade laws that create the necessity for the building to step back as it gains height are in force in this zone.

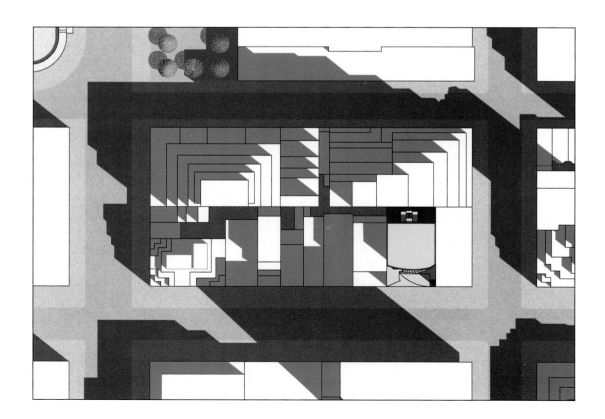

The development
of the project shown
through successive
scale models.

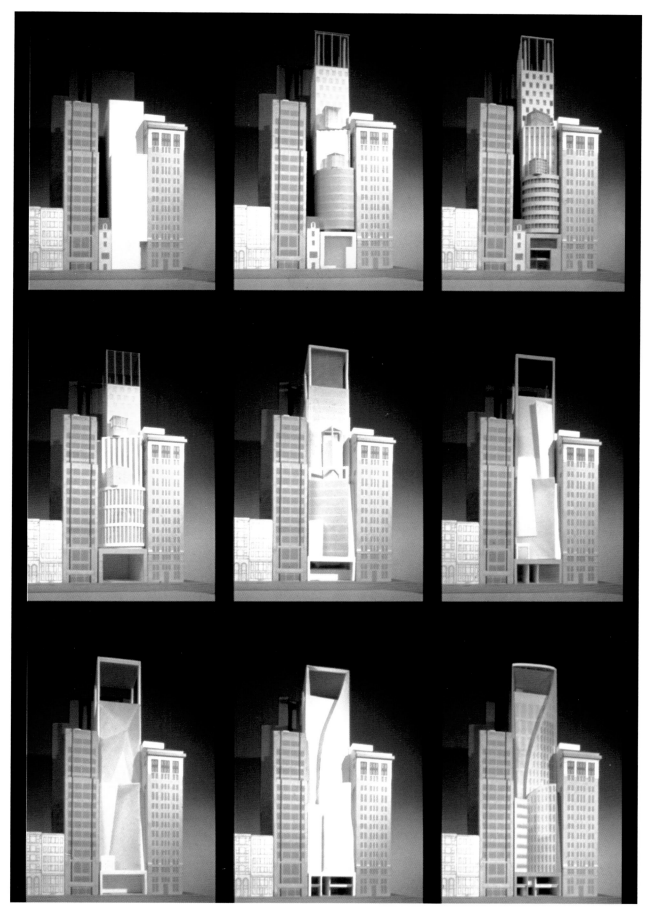

Richard Rogers was born in Florence (Italy) in 1933 and trained to as an architect in England and the United States. He is well known as a pioneer for his buildings (Center Georges Pompidou in Paris, Lloyd's and the Millennium Dome in London and the European Court of Human Rights in Strasbourg), he is one of the world's most outstanding architects and he is the principal counselor in architecture and urban development to the Mayors of London and Barcelona. He has been rewarded with the gold medal of the Royal Institute of British Architects. He was knighted in 1991 and made a life peer in 1996.

R. Rogers, J. Young, M. Goldschmied and M. Davies founded the studio Richard Rogers Partnership in 1977. They have offices in London, Tokyo and Barcelona with a staff of a hundred and thirty people. The work is organized around weekly meetings of the teams responsible for each of the projects. This is a methodology that is maintained throughout the entire process of designing a building. They are pioneers in the field of environmental construction and they have worked on a great variety of projects: public (the courts at Antwerp and Bordeaux), private (three buildings in Potsdamer Platz, Berlín and the VR Techno Plaza, Gifu, Japan), cultural centers, airports (Terminal s1 and 5 at Heathrow) and large-scale master planning projects (Greenwich Peninsula, England).

www.rrp.co.uk

1977	Centre Pompidou, Paris (in collaboration with Renzo Piano)
1986	Lloyd's Office Building, London
1992	Marseilles' International Airport
1995	The European Court of Human Rights, Strasbourg
1996	Office Building at 88 Wood Street, London
2000	Montevideo Residential Complex, Battersea (London)
2000	Central Offices for the Lloyd's Register of Shipping
2001	General Plan for Viladecans Business Park Barcelona (in collaboration with Alonso–Balaguer)
2004	Hotel Hesperia, Barcelona (in collaboration with Alonso–Balaguer)
2007	Project for Terminal 5 for Heathrow Airport

RICHARD ROGERS
Richard Rogers Partnership

Architect:

RICHARD ROGERS PARTNERSHIP

Developers:

Inmobiliaria Espacio, Group Villar Mir

Structural Engineering:

Ove Arup & Partners

Situation:

Madrid, Spain

Project Date:

2002 (competition)

Floors:

45

Height:

214.40 meters

Use:

Offices

Photography:

Richard Rogers Partnership

This project is included in the official plan for "Madrid Arena" which contemplates the construction of four towers, a multi-use pavilion and a large park. The real estate company Espacio held a competition for the design of its corporate headquarters which are to be situated on the northern plot. The building proposed by Richard Rogers Partnership depicts a scheme that best fulfils the client's requirements. In the first place, it follows the overall objective of building a structure that adds vitality to its surroundings. The proposal is a building with a range of interior and exterior spaces where social and leisure activities can be developed as much by the regular users as by visitors. In second place, it fulfills the objectives of creating an office environment with high quality flexible spaces. The proposal is for a building that comes to terms with function, space, movement and construction. Finally, the design responds to the objectives of developing a building that will endure, is moderate in terms of energy consumption and that entails relatively low maintenance costs; environmentally, an effective building that uses a high proportion of low energy materials and that promotes a passive energy culture.

Architecturally, the building assumes the form of frames set in an 'A' shape that shore up the building and is essentially the expression of a tower as a projecting vertical. The apparent simplicity of this form integrates a sophisticated synthesized disposition of the vertical communication and service systems that permits a flexible organization of the office spaces which are totally open to the unhindered views of the city and its surroundings.

The spatial organization of the building is based on the Kantian concept (term from the North American architect Louis I. Kahn who developed the concept) of "spaces served" (that are formed by the occupied floors) and the "spaces that serve" (that provide the essential support that allow the floors to operate) which are expressed by the form and composition of the building. Each group of eight floors forms a "village". Between each of these, a floor,

TORRE ESPACIO

double in height to the rest, has been created to house services and common activity areas such as restaurants, gymnasiums or conference rooms and to define the nature of the building as being a series of "villages situated vertically one on top of the other". On the ground floor, a netlike rectangular matrix has been proposed to fuse the public space (proposed within the official development) and tie the four towers in with the pavilion. From this level, access to the interior of the building is available. Here entrance controls, elements of the vertical communication system and an extensive public space with a covered gallery complete with shopping facilities, cafeterias and exhibitions areas are found.

The enveloping exterior of the building requires a variety of technical solutions in response to its differing orientations to the sun that are manifested in differing compositions all of which respond to a final unitary design. The final design attempts to apply a straightforward form of language and to emphasis the functional requirements as a concept within the outer casing. The design integrates the installations and the concrete structure. Upon exposure the thermal mass provided absorbs the increases in temperature which reduces the demand on the cooling systems and, therefore, saves energy. The building confronts the three aspects of a sustainable design: environment, economy and social responsibility. This has been done by tackling the question of environmental impact by designing the building's systems in such a way as to maximize the use of resources and to obtain reduced energy consumption, and by taking the comfort of the occupants and their satisfaction in the workplace into consideration.

Bottom left. South elevation that cuts through the basement-parking lot. As this is one of the facades that receives most sun, each floor, made of prefabricated white concrete panels, has been aligned in such a way that it projects over the area below and functions like a "brise soleil" and casts shade on the floor beneath.
Bottom right. A view towards the south from the upper floors of the building where the senior executives' offices of the Villar Mir group are located. They are unique due to the inclusion of a garden at this high level over which a meeting room conceived as a suite and located in a glass cone has been hung.

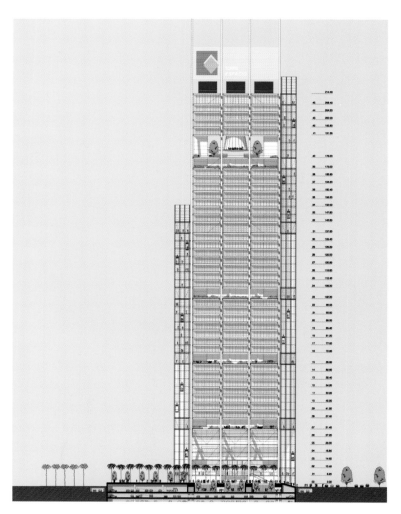

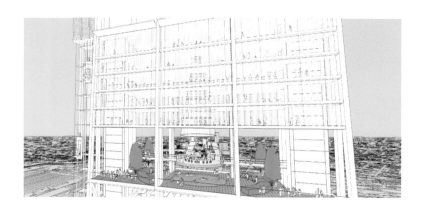

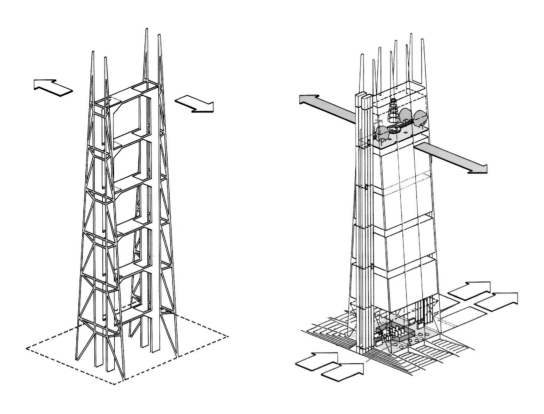

Top from left to right. Schemes that show the main elements of the building such as the east-west stabilizing structure or the direct access to the higher floors where the Villar-Mir group offices are situated.
Bottom from left to right. West elevation and photograph of the scale model. The building's exterior casing requires a variety of claddings to fulfill aesthetic and behavioral criteria.

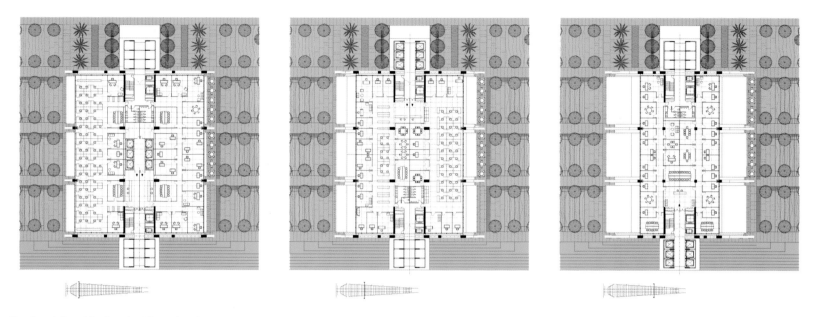

Top from left to right. Standard floor plans for the stories in the low, middle and upper bands of the building. The variation in the scheme for the standard floor plan affects the surface of the floors (they get smaller as the tower gets higher). The distribution of communications and services of each band conforms to a hypothetical central axis that runs parallel to the north and south facades. In all cases, the floors can be distributed according to the tenants' necessities.

Bottom. Ground floor where security controls, some stores and the entrances to the tower by means of elevators and escalators that lead to a platform suspended in space are located. The tower has been placed perpendicular to the Paseo de la Castellana and proposes a facade with rectangular-grid openings that fuses with the buildings included in the General Plan. This matrix could be reinforced with the creation of a new park in which the vegetation could be organized in regular spaces with a north-south orientation interrupted with more natural forms of landscape set in an east-west direction.

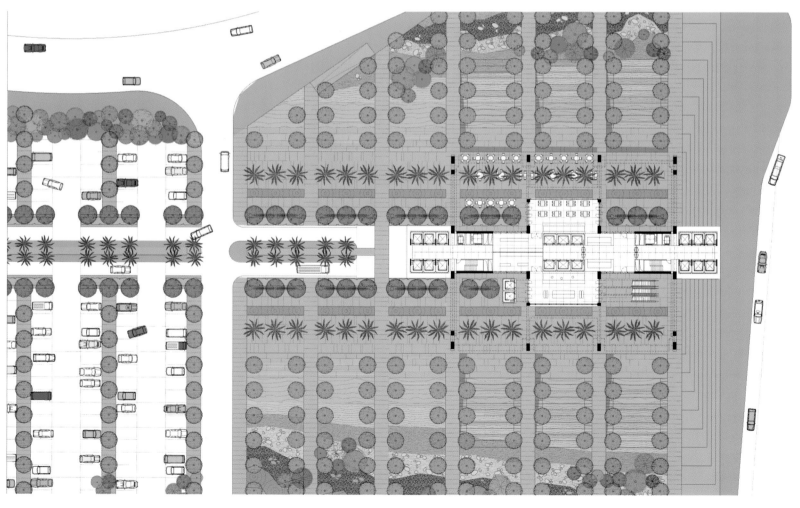

166

Top. Schemes for air conditioning systems that use the separating floors and vaulted concrete ceilings for cooling. The design integrates the installation with the structure.
Bottom. View of the ground floor entrance. This has been projected as a dynamic space generated from a flexion of the north and south facades which creates a "gallery space" on the same axis as the extension of the park.
In the foreground, the escalators that lead to the raised lobby.

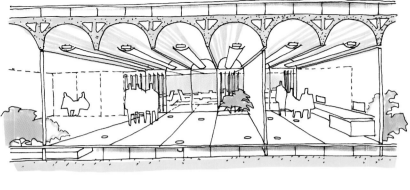

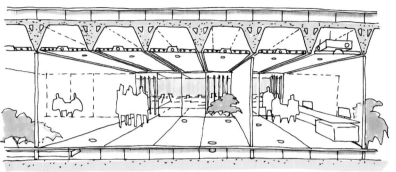

TORRE ESPACIO

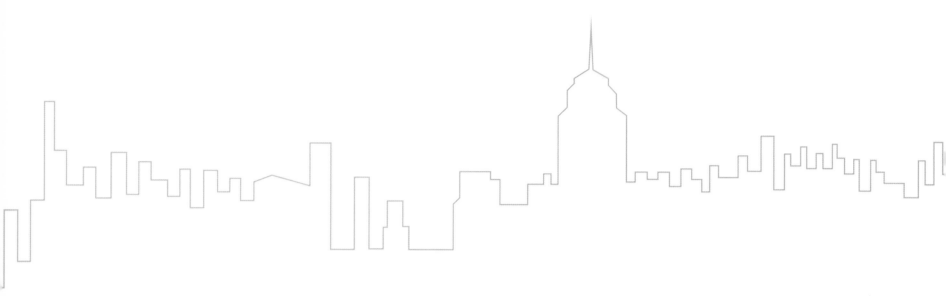

Richard Rogers was born in Florence (Italy) in 1933 and trained to as an architect in England and the United States. He is well known as a pioneer for his buildings (Center Georges Pompidou in Paris, Lloyd's and the Millennium Dome in London and the European Court of Human Rights in Strasbourg), he is one of the world's most outstanding architects and he is the principal counselor in architecture and urban development to the Mayors of London and Barcelona. He has been rewarded with the gold medal of the Royal Institute of British Architects. He was knighted in 1991 and made a life peer in 1996.

R. Rogers, J. Young, M. Goldschmied and M. Davies founded the studio Richard Rogers Partnership in 1977. They have offices in London, Tokyo and Barcelona with a staff of a hundred and thirty people. The work is organized around weekly meetings of the teams responsible for each of the projects. This is a methodology that is maintained throughout the entire process of designing a building. They are pioneers in the field of environmental construction and they have worked on a great variety of projects: public (the courts at Antwerp and Bordeaux), private (three buildings in Potsdamer Platz, Berlín and the VR Techno Plaza, Gifu, Japan), cultural centers, airports (Terminals 1 and 5 at Heathrow) and large-scale master planning projects (Greenwich Peninsula, England).

www.rrp.co.uk

1977	Centre Pompidou, Paris (in collaboration with Renzo Piano)
1986	Lloyd's Office Building, London
1992	Marseilles' International Airport
1995	The European Court of Human Rights, Strasbourg
1996	Office Building at 88 Wood Street, London
2000	Montevideo Residential Complex, Battersea (London)
2000	Central Offices for the Lloyd's Register of Shipping
2001	General Plan for Viladecans Business Park Barcelona (in collaboration with Alonso–Balaguer)
2004	Hotel Hesperia, Barcelona (in collaboration with Alonso–Balaguer)
2007	Project for Terminal 5 for Heathrow Airport

Luis Alonso and Sergi Balaguer, after graduating from the *Escola Tècnica Superior d'Arquitectura de Barcelona* (ETSAB), established themselves professionally in Barcelona in 1978. Since then, they have undertaken more than 600 projects ranging from family homes, promoted both publicly and privately, to sports clubs in which they have introduced concepts of bioclimatic and environmental architecture.

They are currently working in association with the studio Richard Rogers Partnership with whom they are jointly developing projects such as the *Gran Hotel Hesperia* (l'Hospitalet de Llobregat, Barcelona), the leisure center Las Arenas (Barcelona) and the Office Park (Viladecans, Barcelona).

This studio is an example of Catalonian architecture which is radical in thought and versatile in its designs. Their approach to projects is modern and innovative, adventurous and organized. Their concern for social and urban development is reflected by the mentions and prizes they have received for the residential complexes that they have proposed. Their projects range from the smallest of buildings to the most prestigious complexes.

www.alonsobalaguer.com

1992	Sports Club Arsenal, Barcelona
1992	Family Residence, Padua
1998	Apartment Building Nus de la Trinitat, Barcelona
1998	Apartment Building Poble Nou, Barcelona
1999	Hotel Arc de Monells, Monells (Girona, Spain)
2001	Sports Club Balthus, Santiago de Chile
2002	Wellness Center 02, Barcelona
2002	Sports Club Metrópolis, Seville
2003	Residential Tower Illa del Cel, Diagonal Mar, Barcelona
2003	Hotel Caribe, Port Aventura, Salou (Spain)

RICHARD ROGERS
Richard Rogers Partnership

ALONSO-BALAGUER
i Arq.Associats S.L.

RICHARD
ALONSO

Architect:

RICHARD ROGERS PARTNERSHIP + ALONSO-BALAGUER I ARQUITECTES ASSOCIATS

Developers:

Hotels Hesperia

Structural Engineering:

Buro Happold / Obiol, Moya i Associats

Situation:

Hospitalet of Llobregat (Catalonia, Spain)

Project Date:

1999

Completion Date:

2004

Floors:

30

Height:

105 meters

Use:

Hotel, offices and services

Photography:

Richard Rogers Partnership + Melon Studio

Situated in a new urban park, the Gran Hotel Hesperia **** fits into an urbanistic operation that has as its objective the conversion of the beginning of la avenida de la Gran Via de Les Corts Catalanes in the city of Hospitalet de Llobregat (10km from Barcelona and Catalonia's second city in terms of number of inhabitants) into a boulevard integrated into the city. At present, it functions as a freeway used by hundreds of cars every day given that it provides a direct connection between the airport and the center of Barcelona. This is to be transformed into an urban avenue where vehicles and pedestrians coexist and for this a network of facilities and services is being developed such as the Gran Hotel Hesperia that will be the new gateway to the city.

The twenty-two-floor tower accommodates 304 rooms, 16 suites (duplex apartments that are situated on the two last floors), the central offices of the company Hesperia and, as a crowning, a glazed dome where a restaurant with panoramic views is located. In a horizontal volume of a lesser height, at the foot of the tower and parallel to la Gran Vía, a congress palace, a sports center, various restaurants and an underground parking lot are located. Exteriorly, the two buildings form a unique volume. In the interior, continuity between the two structures is given by means of an inclined glass plane which covers part of the vestibule of the lower floors where the public areas of the hotel and the center of conventions are connected. Below the glass roof, various canvases in the form of sails generate shadows in the interior of this great public space that extends uninterruptedly for the spectator throughout the three buildings (hotel, convention center and sports center) and park.

The main facades show the structure and the interior functioning of the building in three strata: the hall of the hotel on the ground floor at its double height, the offices of the company Hesperia occupying the five following floors and an installations floor that sections the building separating the

HOTEL HESPERIA

main body of twenty floors in which the hotel rooms are located. As a topping, the glass dome that accommodates the restaurant bestows a futuristic air and a symbolic character on the building.

The lateral facades have disappeared as such and are the places where the vertical communications nuclei, stairs and elevators, which have been expelled from the interior of the floors, have been located. This gesture is constant in the architecture of Richard Rogers and it allows him to project floors free of obstacles that interfere visually and with spatial distribution. In this way, he has greater liberty when it comes to distributing functions within the interior of a building. The Center d'Art Contemporanie Georges Pompidou in Paris and Lloyd's Bank in London have been two of his previous experiments. Rogers is one of the founders of the High Tech movement in architecture. His work reflects a machine vocation in his buildings which are conceived as technology at the service of people and their welfare.

Scale model and main elevation of the building corresponding to an east-west orientation. From its composition, a functional reading can be established: a public ground floor, a mass of offices and the remainder of the floors destined to a hotel.

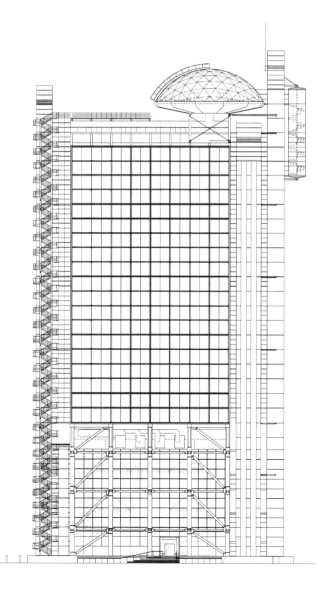

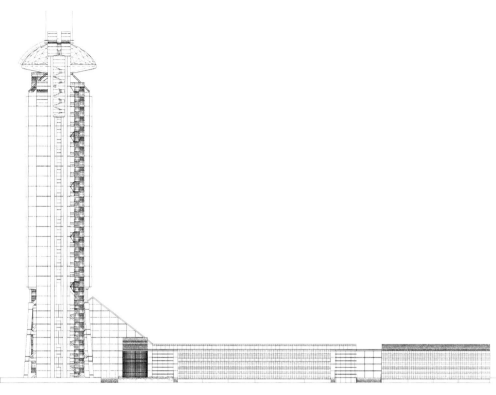

Left. Side elevation which presents the Gran Hotel Hesperia complex in all its full dimensions: a group of buildings that form a unit. Bottom. Photograph of the scale model that details the building's crowning: two floors on which duplex apartments and the glazed cupola are located.

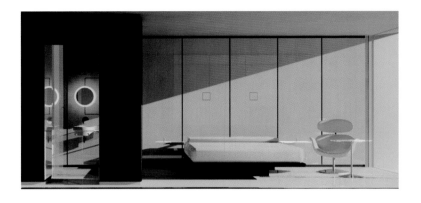
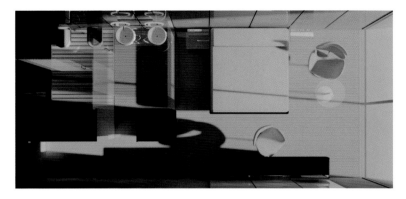

Interior views of a standard room in the hotel. In them, we can see the distribution and some of the final finishes, materials, colors, furniture and illumination. The rooms incorporate the bathroom unit as part of the furniture by replacing the traditional partition wall with a lamina of glass. This mechanism increases the sensation of space within the room and allows the outside to be seen which favors the views. The building has been set perpendicular to the freeway with the intention of diminishing the noise of the traffic and the possibility of any visual obstacle being created by buildings that may be constructed in the future. This arrangement has also improved the views from the rooms.

174

Top. Site plan for the Gran Hotel Hesperia in the complex Gran Via del Hospitalet de Llobregat. Surrounded by the vegetation of the new Bellvitge Park, these emblematic installations will give a welcome to Hospitalet from its southern access that is the access from the airport. It is a question of a freeway: a direct connection with the center of Barcelona.
Bottom. Standard floor plan for the hotel from level 7 to 23. The vertical communications nuclei have been moved to the exterior of the building to facilitate the distribution of each floor.

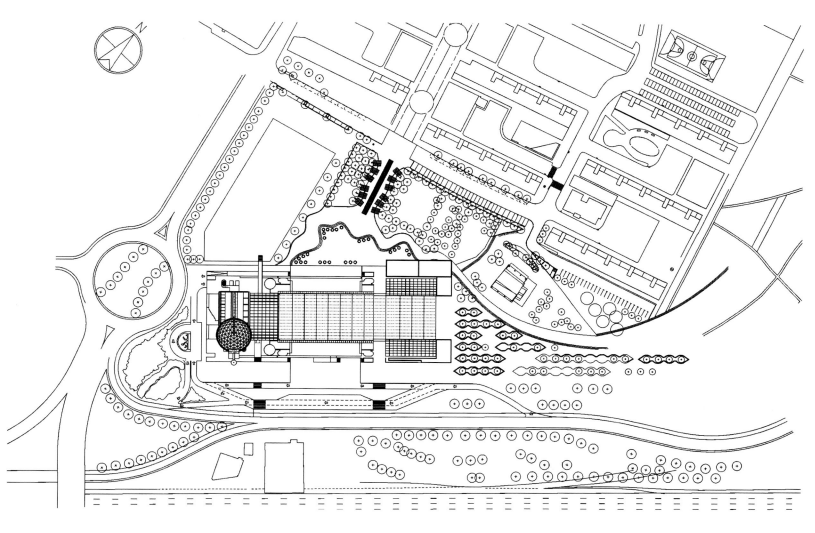

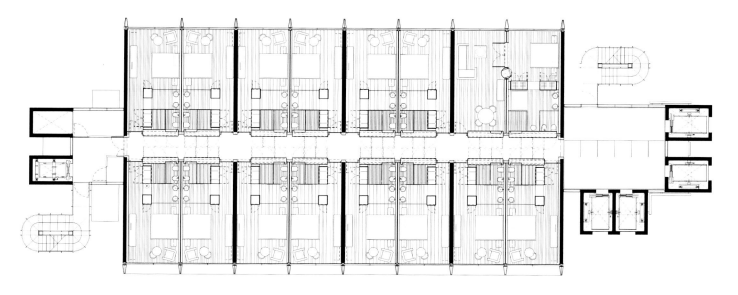

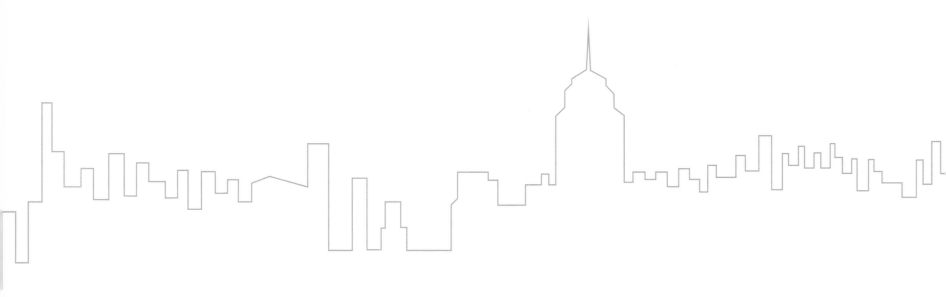

The Japanese firm Nikken Sekkei, based in Osaka, was inaugurated at
the beginning of 1900. It was established as the design/construction su-
pervision section of the Japanese conglomerate "Sumitomo Head Office". In 1933, as a result of reorganization, it became know as "Hasebe,
Takekoshi and Associates, Inc." and later, in 1956, as it is known at
present, Nikken Sekkei Ltd. It counts on affiliated companies such as
the Nikken Housing System, Nikken Soil Research and Nikken Space
Design.

With a total of 1,700 employees distributed among its offices in Nagoya,
Osaka and Tokyo and its external headquarters in China, Korea, Malaya
and Taiwan, this is one of the most important studios dedicated to architecture, urban planning, engineering, consulting and management in
the entire world. The company has completed more than 14,000 projects in over 40 countries that include retail centers, governmental buildings, schools, factories, hospitals and apartment blocks.

The philosophy of the studio is to create sound and progressive designs that are in harmony with their surroundings.

The architect Hideyuki Yokyoa joined the company more than 20 years
ago and he has been the principal designer of two of the most outstanding skyscrapers that the firm has built in China: the Shanghai
Pudong International Finance Building (2000) and the Shanghai Information Center (Pudong, 2002). These two projects reflect the firm's
spectacular high-tech esthetics.

www.nikkensekkei.com

1966	Central Offices for the 114th Bank, Kagawa
1978	Art Museum, Hiroshima
1982	Branch of the Bank of Japan, Osaka
1990	Toyota Auto Salon, Amlux (Tokyo)
1991	Cultural Center for Investigation and Exhibitions, Dunhuang
1994	Kansai International Airport, Osaka (in collaboration with Renzo Piano)
1995	Osaka World Trade Center, Osaka
1996	Sendai Airport Passenger Terminal (Miyagi)
1997	Shihlin Electric Tower, Taipei
2001	Shanghai Information Center, Shangai

HIDEYUKI YOKYOA
Nikken Sekkei LTD.

NIKKEN SEKK

Architect:

NIKKEN SEKKEI LTD

Developers:

Osaka World Trade Center

Structural Engineering:

Obayashi Corporation

Situation:

Technoport Osaka, Osaka (Japan)

Completion Date:

1995

Floors:

55

Height:

256 meters

Use:

Offices and services

Photography:

Kouji Okamoto

Technoport Osaka, where the Osaka World Trade Center (OWTC) building is sited, is a recently constructed urban center on the Bay of Osaka. It extends over an area of 775 hectares divided into three artificial islands. 256 meters high with a total constructed area of 150,000 m2 distributed over 55 floors, this building (the highest in the west of Japan in the year of its construction) has been erected in a short period of time as an outstanding element on the coastline. It is also an outstanding landmark in the Bay of Osaka and Kansai region.

The functional scheme for the OWTC includes various private and public uses. The exterior view of the tower and its cross-section clearly express this functional distribution in which the large space where public activities take place is situated in the podium. On top we find 32 floors which are, with the exception of the last 10 that are smaller, distributed identically for offices and, finally, the crowning. In reality, the building is composed of three sub-buildings with differing geometry.

The ground floor in the base of the tower is characterized by a 3,000-m2 lobby that distributes the public by means of four main banks of glazed elevators that permit, due to their transparency, complete vision of the interior. Behind these, the majority of the public spaces of the building such as stores, restaurants, cafés, the OWTC Club and an auditorium are located. The section of this space reminds us of a pavilion as large beams that allow for an absence of pillars in the interior support the undulating roof. Glass dominates a large part of the facade that creates a luminous space with a great sensation of amplitude. The transition between the base and column has been resolved by the liberation of the first six floors of the tower that leaves only the impressive structure of the inclined pillars that stem from the vestibule. Three basement floors of parking and other services are found underground.

Different uses are embraced in a global design that conceives the area as a central park facing Cosmos Square that links it to the interior. The use of

OSAKA WORLD TRADE CENTER

the vestibule is not limited to the building itself; it also integrates the complete complex into its urban surroundings as much as in function as in scale.

The sixth to the thirty-eighth floor are dedicated to offices. They are functional with a clear distribution to be able to respond to the varying necessities of the different entities that the building may accommodate. The ground floor is rectangular and the elevator banks are aligned in the center freeing the perimeter of the main facades. In the lateral facades, some elements that contain services and the vertical emergency communications nuclei are situated.

The facades are glass planes interrupted by lines of pillars that, in pairs, mark the structure until their arrival at the base of the tower where they incline and intersect with the entrance pavilion. At the top of the building, an inverted pyramid, oriented to the four cardinal points and rotated 45 degrees with regard to the tower, accommodates the remaining public functions. These include banquet halls, convention halls, various restaurants, the OWTC museum and a spectacular panoramic gallery with an inclined facade from where a good part of the bay and the surroundings of Osaka can be made out. During the night, the OWTC appears as a great tower of light with this 'observation bridge' crowning the building.

Top. Image of the spacious ground floor that forms the base of the tower, a lobby and a large public space.
Bottom left. Interior view of the lobby. The structure of the tower situated in the facade plane is not perpendicular to the plane of the ground at ground-floor level. It is inclined at 45° and incorporated into the lobby thus, uniting both constructions (the tower and the podium). This gesture, which evokes images of buttresses, is also perceived from the outside.
Bottom right. Floor plan of the square-floored body that tops the tower and in which a panoramic viewing point has been installed.

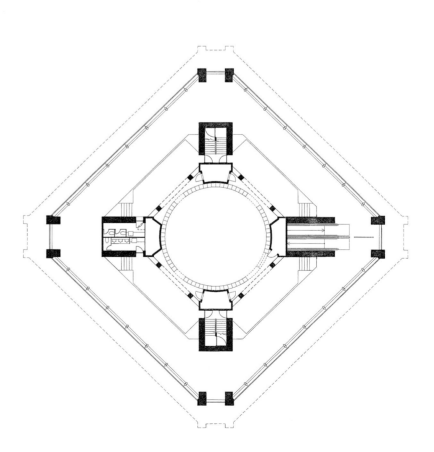

Top. Photograph of one of the upper floors of offices. The facade is a glass curtainwall which is only interrupted by the structure of the building. Bottom. Photograph of the panoramic viewing point which is an inverted pyramid oriented to the cardinal points of the compass and rotated at 45° to the axis of the tower.

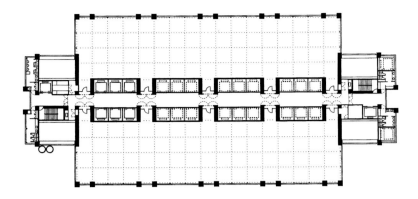
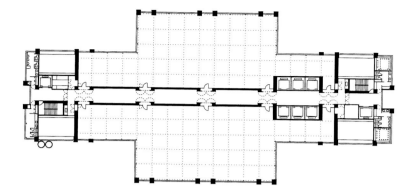

Top left. Standard floor plan of the floors designated to offices. Rectangular in shape, they are organized along a longitudinal axis that distributes the elevator banks and various symmetrical rigid outer nuclei. The higher floors have a smaller surface area and are topped by the panoramic viewing point.
Bottom. Photograph of the OWTC and its immediate surroundings.
Cross-section of the tower which shows the levels underground, the structure, and the continuity of the ground floor between the tower and its base.

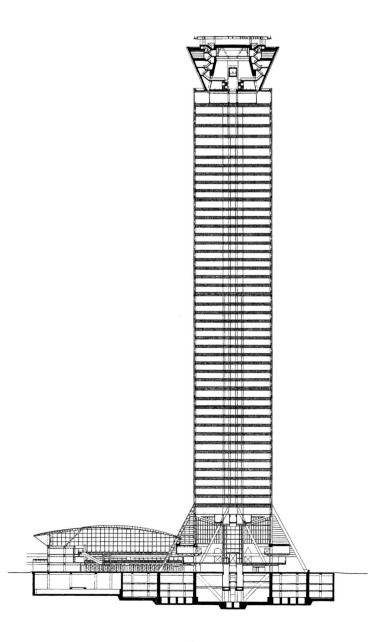

Top. Shot of the elevator banks in the ground floor lobby. One of the predominant elements of this large public space is the light. In order to obtain a bright and airy atmosphere, one part of the structure moves, leaving the elevator cabins and the outer glass casing on view.
Bottom. Osaka World Trade Center photographed from the sea. It is an emblematic building of the recently developed district of the Technoport and a reference for Osaka's marine facade.

Architect:

NIKKEN SEKKEI LTD

Developers:

Shanghai Information World Company Ltd

Structural Engineering:

Nikken Sekkei Ltd

Situation:

Shanghai (The People's Republic of China)

Project Date:

1998

Completion Date:

2001

Floors:

41

Height:

285 meters

Use:

Offices and services

Photography:

Shinkenchiku-sha

During the last decade a large number of skyscrapers have been constructed in Shanghai, concentrated in the Pudong area, which is recognizable from a distance by the forest of towers of which it is composed. This reflects the economic expansion and political swing that the country has experienced which, along with the rapid acceptance of consumerism in Asia at large, has changed the communist culture.

In 1990, the Chinese government declared Pudong (the most prosperous district of the city situated along the river Huangpu next to the old district and historical avenue Bund) a "Special Economic Zone" and established that it was to be an area of free commerce in order to encourage foreign investment.

With the advantages of being able to count on large resources, economic privileges and the favorable geographical situation of the city, foreign operators decided to invest in the Shanghai market. In contrast, the administration imposes strict controls on the foreign architectural studios that design the headquarters for these large corporations. As a result of the philosophy of the communist regime, which does not permit the development of the private enterprise, these architects have to associate themselves with local studios that take on the execution phase of the projects and direct the works.

The Shanghai Information Center is an Asian building that has been conceived by Asian architects and is also closely linked to the technological culture. The desire of the developers was to construct a building that reflected the evolution of the local telecommunications sector in the China of the 21st century.

This expressive image extracted from the dynamic context in which the building is situated – in the heart of the Pudong Development Area, surrounded by high-rise buildings, large masses that block the views in all directions – has

SHANGHAi INFORMATION CENTER

Top. Exterior photograph of the lower part of the tower taken at night that features the lobby, a great public space approximately seven floors high.
Bottom left. Exterior view of the building along with other constructions that have recently been completed in the City of Shanghai.
Bottom right. The main entrance to the ground floor lobby.

obliged it to determine its own place. It also represents the gateway to Pudong as a consequence of the symbolic character that the developers wished to bestow upon the building.

Among its main uses we find an integrated complex of offices, technical spaces for telecommunications (at a regional level) with executive and administrative offices, office space for rent and the Museum of Information and Telecommunications.

Once the spatial problems of housing these functions were resolved, it was decided to give the building a human scale by introducing a public use to the ground floors. This has been presented as a spacious atrium which is 35m high, completely transparent and free from obstacles. This has only been interrupted by the presence of mechanical stairs situated in a corner that transport visitors to the sphere suspended from the roof that introduces them into a magical world.

The floors are completely clear and the communications nuclei and services have been displaced toward the sides where the telecommunication systems are located. The concrete pillar structure has been modeled so as to form three zones, a central one that receives the greatest use and two (with more light) in the perimeter of the facade.

The exterior image of the Shanghai Information Center is the reflection of its interior in as much as the facades express, with volumetric rotundity, the differing functions in two differentiated readings. The horizontal strips of glass and aluminum form the covering of the telecommunications zones, and a reflective glass curtainwall encases the floors of office space. In the purity of this prism, the transparency of the ground floor and the telecommunication antenna stand out. This emphasizes the verticality of the building and converts it into an icon of the Shanghai of the telecommunications.

Interior views of the lobby. The facade is a glass plane that not only protects the interior, but also makes it constantly visible. The interior is a large dynamic space in which the visitor comes across different volumes, ramps and so on that appear to float in the immense space.

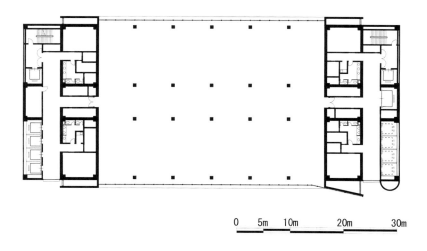

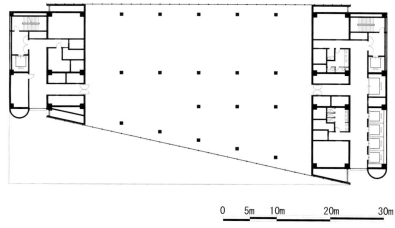

Top from left to right. Standard floor plans for the tower. The first section is rectangular while the higher floors have a smaller surface area and a facade that is inclined diagonally with respect to the body of the building. Spatially, the floors are organized according to the rhythm that is created by the structure and leave a longitudinal central passageway as an axis that organizes the services and communications nuclei perpendicularly in the lateral facades.

Bottom. Longitudinal section of the tower and photograph taken from the outside. The antenna that tops the building is both a technical and a formal element.

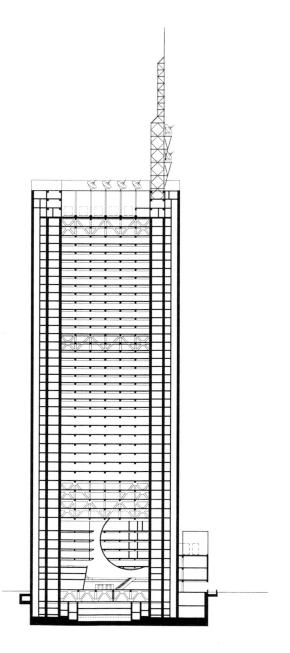

Top. Location and ground floor level in which the space created can be read as a large and totally transparent lobby with services and communications nuclei on either side. An independent staircase that leads to the great sphere that hangs from the ceiling is the only element that interrupts this space.
Bottom. Detail of the steel and glass pergola that covers the main entrances to the ground floor.

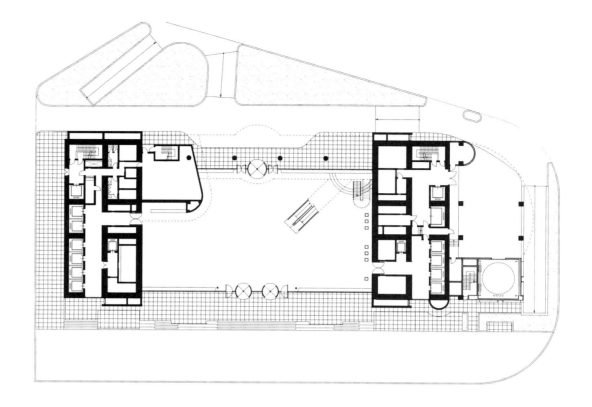

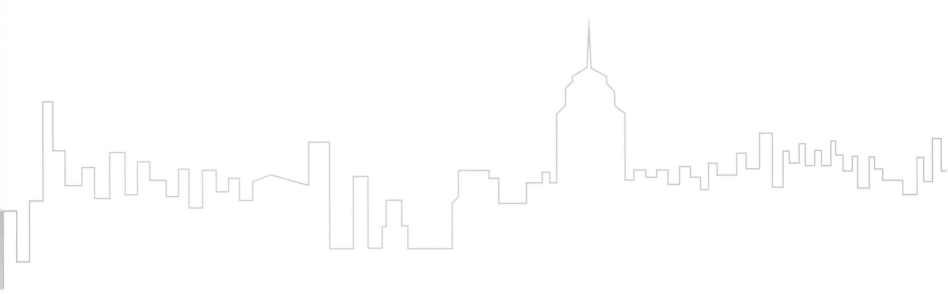

Tengku Robert Hamzah and Ken Yeang founded the firm of architecture T.R. Hamzah & Yeang Sdn Bhd in Kuala Lumpur in 1976. At present, more than fifty people distributed among the first headquarters of the Malaysian capital, Pudang, and other cities of Australia, China and Singapore work for the firm. Both associates studied architecture in English universities. This is a tradition in Malaysia where American architecture is not a point of reference.

Ken Yeang graduated in the Architectural Association School of London and took his doctor's degree at Cambridge University with a thesis that investigated the ecological factors in urban surroundings. He is an architect who is well known for his theoretical work. This he has transmitted as much through his books (for example the influential titles Designing with Nature and The Skyscraper: Bioclimatically Considered) as by the buildings he has built in the southeast of Asia over the last fifteen years into which he has constantly integrated his principles of ecological construction.

www.trhamzahyeang.com

1992	Office Building Menara Mesiniaga, Selangor
1996	Office Building Central Plaza, Kuala Lumpur
1998	Office Building Menara Umno, Penang
1998	Guthrie Pavilion, Selangor
2000	Project for Al Asima Shopping Village Complex, Kuwait
2000	Project for an Ecological Residential Tower in Elephant & Castle (London)
2002	Millenium Monument, Putrajaya
2003	The Technological Design Center of Malaysia, Cyberjaya (Selangor)
2004	Project for the New National Library, Singapore
2005	Project for the tower for Expo Nagoya 2005

DR. KEN YEANG
T.R. Hamzah & Yeang Sdn Bhd

T.R. HAM

Architect:

T.R. HAMZAH & YEANG SDN BHD

Developer:

Salhia Real Estate Company K.S.C.

Structural Engineering:

Battle McCarthy Consulting

Situation:

Kuwait (Kuwait)

Project Date:

2000 (competition)

Floors:

40

Height:

157.5 meters

Use:

Offices and retail

Photography:

T.R. Hamzah & Yeang Sdn. Bhd

Al Asima Shopping Village is a complex for mixed uses formed of different types of buildings. It consists of an office tower and other lower buildings which form a base in which four additional floors of offices and three more that contain a retail area forming a podium have been arranged. One of the client's requirements was that the typology of the retail center was to relate to the American concept of a *mall*. The proposal presented by the architect Ken Yeang's team presents a Retail Village as an alternative to a classical mall. The *Al Asima Shopping Village* stands out for the way in which it incorporates elements that are characteristic of a traditional village of the area.

The complex will be like a large bazaar that offers different itineraries and places which form their own identities. The point of reference for the complex is the tower which identifies it and fixes its position in space. In the base, the different building are organized around a central square. Each one of these buildings is like a village. Each village is a construction in the form of a ring that is created around a central public space and a landscaped plaza covered with large skylights. The visitor to the complex will have the sensation of inhabiting an exterior public space as it is illuminated in a natural way and does not give the sensation of timelessness produced by a closed building. All the villages are communicated one with another by means of pedestrian walkways and, on the lower floors, wide interior streets with glazed roofs have been created. The glass, in addition to providing a certain amount of protection from the sun, is one of the materials that unifies the complex as it extends over the lower buildings like a skin that finally covers the tower as well.

The integration of vegetation into the interior of the buildings where small gardens have been created responds to this idea of combining the exterior and interior and to creating rest areas for pedestrians and office users. The same mechanism has also been used in the office tower where a gar-

den, covered by an arch that is a prolongation of the facade, has been situated on the roof. This vegetation not only helps maintain a comfortable temperature within the building, but it also creates drafts of air that refresh and reduce the humidity that is typical of the climate in Kuwait.

The office tower responds to an architecture that goes beyond contemporary images. Its futurist design desires to respond to the new ideas regarding the design of office buildings and to be a functional and artistic model for the city. The 40 floors are covered with membranes that wrap the structure and protect it from the outside. The rectangular morphology of the floor (also that of the remainder of the complex and the final volume) comes from the world of biology. The main facades are oriented to the north, toward the coast, and to the south, so that the facades with a smaller surface are those oriented to the east and west. This reduces the amount of direct solar radiation and, therefore, the consumption of air-conditioning in the interior of the building.

The architect Ken Yeang has been working in countries in the south of Asia for the last 15 years. He has been working on a series of office buildings in which he has applied his principles of bioclimatic towers. Installations in office buildings are becoming more and more sophisticated and are consuming greater amounts of energy. In the long term, this machinery and a large amount of the materials used in the construction are harmful to people and to the planet. A form of architecture that is more respectful with the planet and its inhabitants can be developed. We are talking about bioclimatic architecture as a discipline based on mechanisms as ancestral as that of a knowledge of nature and its effects over the earth to enable us to distribute spaces and locate a building in a logically way.

The Al Asima Shopping Village project is a complex formed by an office tower, its base and two other buildings. One of these two buildings accommodates offices and the other, a retail center. All the elements of this complex are interrelated and connected as shown in the three different views of the scale model.

Top. The scale model viewed from above. In this photograph, the idea of the complex as a unit is perceived. Bottom. View of the ground floor of the tower in which the vegetation plays an active role. It becomes, simply, another material.

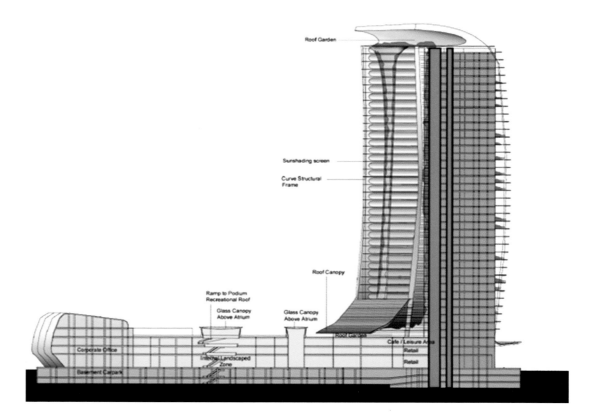

Top. Elevations and sections of the complex.
Bottom. Side view of the scale model that shows the tower and the base of the complex. The way the facade has been treated stands out. The curtainwall, which is like a membrane, only covers part of the skeleton of the tower. The rest remains visible.

196

Top and bottom. Details of the scale model which show the covered walkways that have been created between the different areas of the complex and its coverings. The organic geometry of the volumes does not distinguish between the planes of facade or those of the roofs thanks to a homogenous treatment that is, to an extent, abstract.

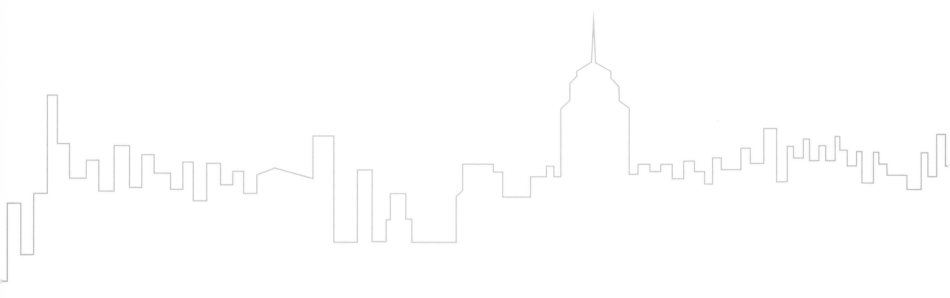

Eberhard H Zeidler is the Founding Partner and Partner-in-Charge of Design of Zeidler Grinnell Partnership/Architects, one of Canada's most internationally renowned firms of architecture and urban development. Their headquarters are in Toronto, but they also have offices in London, Berlin and West Palm Beach.

Eberhard H Zeidler was born in Germany, he graduated in 1948 in the Bauhuaus and in 1949, he took his doctor's degree in the Universität Friderichana (Karlsruhe). In 1951, he emigrated to Canada where he continued his professional career along with the firm Blackwell, Craig & Zeidler which is now called Zeidler Grinnell Partnership/Architects.

He has given various conferences in the School of Architecture and has been assistant lecturer at the Architectural Design which both form part of the University of Toronto. His collaborations include having been a member of the city council's department for urban development and having sat on juries for various cultural and international scientific entities. His designs have been published in national and international specialized magazines and he has written two books: Healing the Hospital (Zeidler, 1974) and Multi Use Architecture in the Urban Context (Kramer Verlag, 1983).

www.zrpa.com

1977	Retail Complex Eaton, Toronto
1986	Leisure-Retail complex Ontario Place, Ontario
1988	The Gallery Complex, Baltimore
1993	The Institute of Cancer of Ontario (Princess Margaret Hospital), Ontario
1995	Columbus Center of Marine Exploration and Investigation, Baltimore
1996	Ontario Science Center Complex, Ontario
1996	Office Building BNI City, Jakarta
1989	Place Montreal Complex, Montreal
1989	Office Building Rogers Campus, Toronto
2002	Office Building Torre Mayor, Mexico D.F.

EBERHARD H. ZEIDLER
Zeidler Grinnell Partnership/Architects

EBERHA
ZEIDL

Architect:

ZEIDLER GRINNELL PARTNERSHIP

Promotor:

ICA Reichmann Torre Mayor

Developers:

The Cantor Seinuk Group P.C., E.Martinez Romero S.A. de C.V.

Situation:

Mexico D. F. (Mexico)

Project Date:

1996

Completion Date:

2002

Floors:

57

Height:

225 meters

Use:

Offices

This building, which at present is in the final phases of construction, will dominate the view of the Parque de Chapultepec in the capital of Mexico. Given that it will be the highest tower in the whole of South America, it has been designed with the city's skyline in mind. It was designed with the most advanced technology to stand and cushion the seismic movements produced in Mexico which is one of the zones with the greatest number of earthquakes in the world. The imposing silhouette is situated at a tangent to the Paseo de la Reforma where the main entrance is found. As the building will be visible form many major points in the city, it is sure to become an important geographical landmark.

The tower has been raised over a base which accommodates two floors of stores and restaurants with direct access to the outside. This element endeavors to relate the tower to other skyscrapers in the area and with the old buildings that still form part of the make-up of the Paseo de la Reforma. Its volume is the result of intersecting two geometric figures: a cylinder and a rectangle each finished in a different way. The facade of the rectangular section of the tower is covered with pink granite and, over this pink background, the windowpanes form positive and negative volumes that produce a grid like composition. In contrast, the curved facade comprises a double-glazed skin that combines panes treated with special dyes so that when reflections fall on its surface, a dynamic vision of this side of the building is created.

The curved shaft of the tower starts and finalizes in different ways. At the top, it doubles back forming an inclined glazed plane under which an atrium, three floors high, is formed that crowns the building. From this space a privileged view of the city can be enjoyed.

The meeting of the tower with the lower floors takes place where the curtainwall steps inwards and forms, through a new plaza, an entrance of

TORRE MAYOR

Top. Digital image of the main entrance to the tower from Paseo de la Reforma. Bottom from left to right. Two views of the building inserted into its urban context. Views from the castle in Chapultepec park and, from the opposite direction, from Paseo de la Reforma towards the Memorial and the Castle. The play between the skin of the rectangular granite volume and cylindrical form of the glass curtainwall will be visible and will change according to the point from which the tower is observed.

grand dimensions. This is the main access to the entrance hall of the building and a great public space that fuses with the podium that has been designed as if it were two lion's paws that embrace and prolong the plaza toward the Paseo de la Reforma. If viewed in perspective from the Castle, which marks the end of the Paseo de la Reforma by means of a visual axis, the intention of the gesture which is produced when the facade arrives at street level can be understood; how it opens to increment the size of the public space in its interior and to expose its structure of concrete pillars. The project concentrates the major part of its effort on bringing the scale of the building closer to the user by means of this entrance.

The architect Eberhard Zeidler, conscience of the impact that a skyscraper has on a city, has worked on this project from a technical and urban point of view giving great importance to the latter aspect. Its great height will be a powerful reference and the play between the rectangular stone volume and the curved glass surface will be visible and changeable as one advances along the Paseo de la Reforma. The podium, designed as if it were two lion's paws that embrace and open the plaza toward the Paseo de la Reforma, is an element that introduces dynamism to the access area where bars and restaurants are found. For pedestrians, the city has gained a new public space, the plaza in front of the building in compensation for the volume created.

Top. Watercolor representing a view of the tower from the park. Standard floor plan that is organized around a central nucleus.
Bottom. Watercolor that shows the entrance to the main lobby from the plaza that lies at a tangent to the pathway in front of the entrance. The homogenous covering of the facade, a composition of horizontal strips of glass and steel, exposes the structure and the interior of the building and becomes a glass skin that draws an arc on the facade.

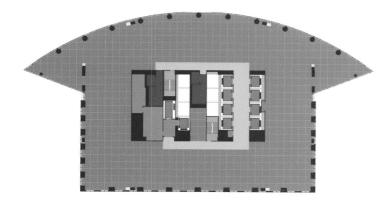

Top left. Detail of the structure on a standard office floor. The concrete pillars, which along with the central nucleus support the building, are tautened by means of metallic struts situated all around the perimeter of the facade. In this way, the behavior of the building in the case of seismic movements will be improved.

Top right. Digital view that shows the interior of the atrium located on the higher floors. Under the inclined plane of the facade a skylight has been created. The higher floors are stepped and a bright and airy area has been created.

Inferior. Axonometric drawing of the element that crowns the tower. The inclined plane of the facade is a technical element of a metallic structure that also controls the excess of the solar radiation.

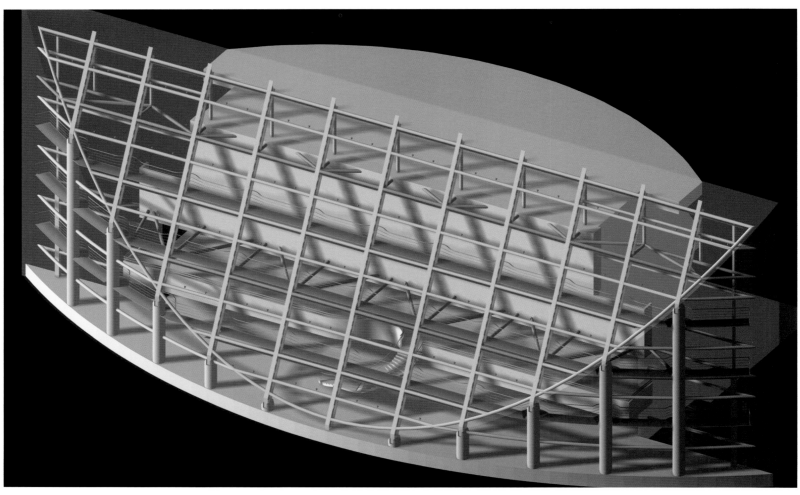

Top. Interior view of the ground floor lobby. This is a large public area with a lot of natural light which, in addition to providing access to the office floors, holds a retail center, bars and restaurants.

Bottom left. The building under construction. Part of the structure for the higher floors is exposed.

Bottom right. West elevation in which the double volume of the tower along with the gestures made in its commencements and in its topping is shown. The ground floor expresses the architect's will to relate the scale of the building to the user through its entrance and that of the building to the Paseo de la Reforma by means of the plaza located in front of the main entrance.

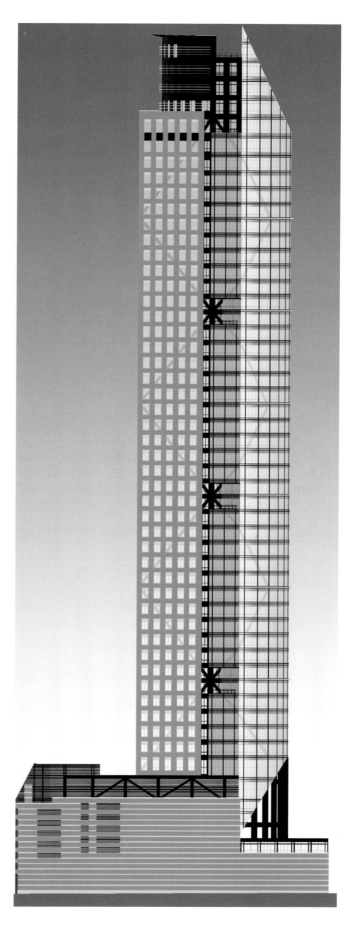

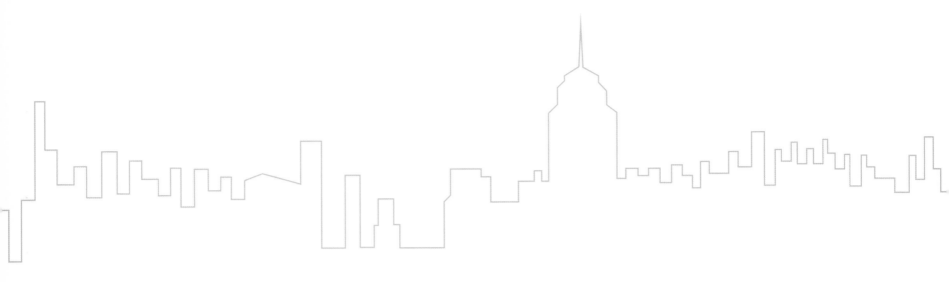

NORR Limited is a full-service architectural and engineering firm located in Toronto. The company was founded in 1938 and since then, it has promoted creativity by developing a commercial brand that guarantees quality at a fair price. It has also contributed many innovative technical solutions thanks to a large professional team that includes H. Wong.

Hazel Wong graduated as an architect in the Carleton University of Ottawa and completed her studies in the Massachusetts Institute of Technology. She has collaborated with Canadian architectural firms and, as an associate of NORR Limited Toronto, she has collaborated in large projects such as Toronto's Pearson International Airport and the Skydome Stadium. She was co-author of the National Bank of Dubai Headquarters and has been responsible for NORR's design department in the Arabian Emirates (UAE) where the Emirates Twin Towers, the Civil Aviation Dubai Headquarters and the United Arab Shipping Company Headquarters have recently been completed.

At present, Hazel Wong develops her professional activity independently in the Arabian Emirates (UAE) and Canada.

www.norrlimited.com

1965	City Hal, Toronto
1989	Office Building Crown Life (phase I), Toronto
1990	Skydome Stadium, Toronto
1991	Rogers Communication Center, Polytechnic University Ryerson, Toronto
1996	Simcoe Building, Toronto
1998	National Bank of Dubai, Dubai
1999	John Sopinka Courthouse, Hamilton (Ontario)
2000	Pavilion Africa Tropical, Toronto Zoo
2000	Torres Emirates, Dubai
2002	Air Canada / Canadian Pacific Consolidation Building, terminals 1 and 2 for Lester B. Pearson International Airport, Toronto

HAZLE WONG
Norr Limited

NORR LIMIT

NORR
LIMIT

Architect:

NORR Limited

Developers:

HH General Sheikh Mohamed
bin Rashid al Maktoum

Structural Engineering:

Hyder Consulting Pty Ltd,
Multiplex Constructions Pty Ltd

Situation:

Dubai (United Arab Emirates)

Project Date:

1997

Completion Date:

2000

Floors:

38 and 55

Altura:

305 and 355 meters

Use:

Offices, hotel and retail

Photography:

Jumeirah International
Hedrich-Blessing Photography

The height and omnipotent presence of their form have transformed the Emirates Towers into the most important landmark in Dubai, the second city (in terms of population and surface area) of the Arabian Emirates. They are situated in the financial district of the city of which they are a symbol of its growing economic power which has made it become an important international business center.

The complex consists of two towers. A 355-meter office tower and another, 305 meters high, that accommodates a luxury hotel. Both have a triangular floor plan and are situated symmetrically upon a horizontal granite podium which is three floors high where shared public functions are carried out within the complex, for example, the Emirates Towers Boulevard. The commercial galleries, bars, restaurants, leisure areas of the hotel and the car parking levels and services are connected via spacious corridors illuminated naturally thanks to skylights and panoramic elevators. The car park, which is located in an adjacent building under a curvilinear structure that evokes the undulating forms of dunes in the desert, has a capacity for 1,800 vehicles.

Inspired by geometric Islamic designs, the predominant element in the composition of the buildings is the triangle. It is apparent in varying levels of detail in the entire project: from the form of the ground plan of the towers, of the roofs, of the skylights, of the structures of the pavilion with the simplified glazed designs repeated on the ceramic tiles along with the interior and exterior pavements. In counterpoint to this rigid geometry and all mixed together are the smooth curves of the structure of the podium, which is covered with granite, the elegant entrance to the retail galleries with the structure of the towers and the great water fountain in front of the main entrance to the hotel that presides and organizes the exterior of the complex.

The main entrance to the office tower has been conceived for wheeled vehicles. It passes over a ramp that accompanies the circular form of the base of the building.

ED

EMIRATES TOWERS

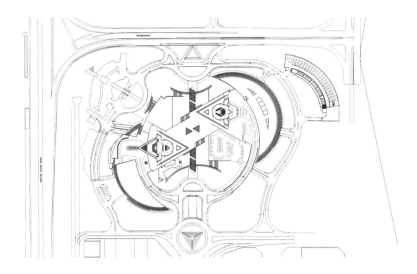

A large triangular pergola dominates the entrance along with two water fountains - a common motif in Islamic culture. The entrance hall is laid out around a central nucleus where elevators are arranged in four units that serve the entire building by zones. The first levels of the towers are geometrically different from the standard floors that are triangular. They function as back-up floors for the hotel's activities, offices and rooms that can be used for conferences. They form a glass cylinder, eight floors high, that creates an extremely high porch on the ground floor. The main entrance to the hotel, and also to the Emirates Towers Boulevard, is situated facing the most important street in the city and is dominated by a grand fountain. The standard floors are organized in a similar way to the office tower. A central body of elevators (four of them with panoramic views) has been laid out around an atrium 31 floors high. The rooms have been distributed around the perimeter of the facade. The last seven floors are communicated by means of three private elevators that serve 57 special rooms for executives, four presidential suites and a restaurant that offers exclusive views of the coast from the highest floor.

The two symmetrical towers are covered with silver-plating and glass. They sparkle by day and, during the night, the artificial lighting reinforces the silhouettes that are raised and culminate in a singular figure. Its slender proportion and the smooth gesture in the final floors, aimed at the heavens and crowned by an aerial, emphasizes the sensation of height and forthrightness that is trimmed in the heavens of the city.

Top. Site plan for the Emirates Towers complex that are dedicated, respectively, to a hotel and offices. In the base, a large leisure-retail complex has been developed that includes restaurants and parking facilities.
Bottom left. Photograph of the complex in which the Emirates Towers Hotel, which forms part of the chain of luxury hotels Jumeirah International, is in the foreground.
Bottom right. Cross-section.

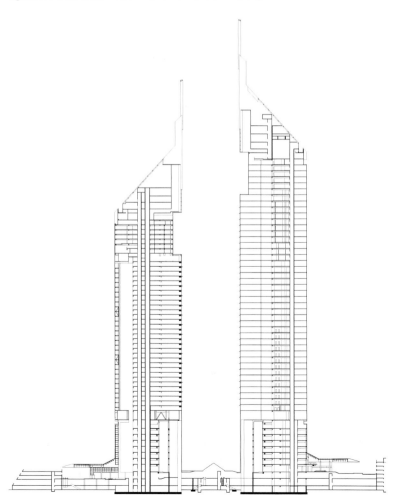

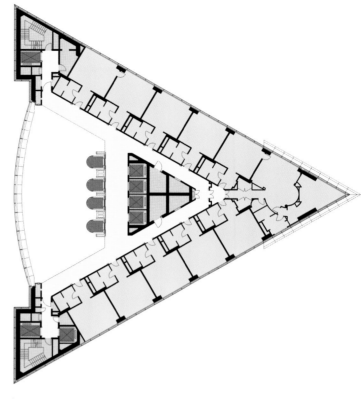

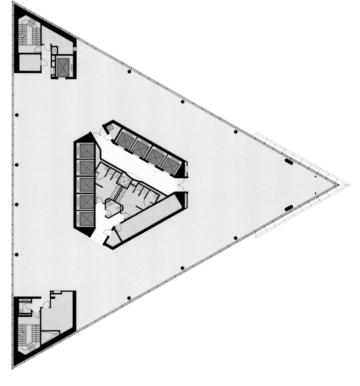

Top and bottom left. Photograph of the towers in the context of the city of Dubai. Their height contrasts with the topography of the city in which the number of skyscrapers has increased over the last few years. Nocturnal view from the street. Top and bottom right. Standard floor plans for the hotel and offices. The floors in both towers are distributed around a central nucleus.

Photographs of the interior of the hotel and the large luminous entrance lobby in which we can see the banks of glazed elevators that move through its large expanse.

Photographs of the interior of the hotel. The central role taken by the natural direct zenithal illumination stands out. It is in the public spaces such as the lobbies and reception areas where vestibules and skylights emphasize the amplitude of the installations.

213

Various views of the towers that are characterized by their volumes, profiles and the play on symmetries that has been established between them. In the Emirates Towers Hotel, the facades stand out with respect to the office tower due to the curved curtainwall. It is the casing of the large central space and, like a cylinder, breaks with the orthogonal geometry of the other two facades.

Formally, the tower is based on a tripartite conception of base, shaft and crowning. The base releases the mass of the building in each of its three vertices among which a glass cylinder has been created. The shaft has two symmetrical facades composed of horizontal strips and a third that is formed by a continuous curtainwall that forms a concave plane in the hotel. Finally, the crown, an inclined plane that fulfils the function of a skylight and that is topped with an antenna.

© Jumeirah International

© Jumeirah International

© Jumeirah International

The publication of this book would not have been possible without the help and support of those, and especially the architects and their teams, who have been directly or indirectly involved in its production. We would like to thank all for their patience, dedication and kindness.

Alonso-Balaguer i Arquitectes Associats (Pau Balaguer, Lluís Alonso)

Atelier Christian de Portzamparc (Gabriella Wilson)

b720 Arquitectura (Fermín Vázquez, Ana Bassat)

Cesar Pelli & Associates Arquitects (César Pelli, Mig Halpine, Lesley Holford)

D. Lau & NG Chun Man Architects & Engineers (Liby Kwok, Shelly Tang)

E. Miralles & B.Tagliabue Arquitectes Associats (Mireia Fornells, Elena Rocchi)

Foster & Partners (Kate Stirling, Pippa Taylor)

Fox & Fowle Architects (Kirsten Sibilia)

Jumeirah International, Emirates Towers Hotel (Marcela Maximova)

Kohn Pedersen Fox Associates PC (Gale Chaney, Elisabeth Austin)

Studio Fuksas (Francesco Colarossi)

Murphy/Jahn Inc Architects (Keith H. Palmer, Lori Hladek)

Nikken Sekkei Ltd. (Naeko Yamamoto)

Norr Limited (Gayle Webber)

Renzo Piano Building Workshop (Stefania Canta)

Richard Rogers Partnership (Jan Güell, Tina Wilson, Robert Torday, David Ardill)

TR Hamzah & Yeang SDN BHD (Dr. Ken Yeang, Yenniu)

Zeidler Grinnell Partnership (Eberhard H. Zeidler, Rosalind Yang)